MY STRIPES
WERE EARNED IN HELL

MY STRIPES
WERE EARNED IN HELL

A French Resistance
Fighter's Memoir of Survival
in a Nazi Prison Camp

Jean-Pierre Renouard

TRANSLATED BY MIMI HORNE

ROWMAN & LITTLEFIELD PUBLISHERS, INC.
Lanham • Boulder • New York • Toronto • Plymouth, UK

Published by Rowman & Littlefield Publishers, Inc.
A wholly owned subsidiary of
The Rowman & Littlefield Publishing Group, Inc.
4501 Forbes Boulevard, Suite 200, Lanham, Maryland 20706
http://www.rowmanlittlefield.com

Estover Road, Plymouth PL6 7PY, United Kingdom

Copyright © 2012 by Jean-Pierre Renouard
English-language translation copyright © 2012 by Mimi Horne
Originally published in French under the title Un costume rayé d'enfer
Copyright © 2008 Éditions Pocket, un département d'Univers Poche

All rights reserved. No part of this book may be reproduced in any form or
by any electronic or mechanical means, including information storage and
retrieval systems, without written permission from the publisher, except by
a reviewer who may quote passages in a review.

British Library Cataloguing in Publication Information Available

Library of Congress Cataloging-in-Publication Data

Renouard, Jean-Pierre.
  [Costume rayé d'enfer. English]
  My stripes were earned in hell : a French resistance fighter's memoir
of survival in a Nazi prison camp / Jean-Pierre Renouard ; translated by
Mimi Horne.
      p.   cm.
  Translation of: Un costume rayé d'enfer. Paris : Pocket, 2008.
  ISBN 978-1-4422-1399-9 (cloth : alk. paper) — ISBN 978-1-4422-
1401-9 (electronic)
  1. Renouard, Jean-Pierre. 2. World War, 1939–1945—Prisoners and
prisons, German. 3. World War, 1939–1945—Concentration camps—
Germany. 4. World war, 1939–1945—Personal narratives, French. 5.
Prisoners of war—Germany—Biography. 6. Prisoners of war—France—
Biography. I. Title.
  D805.G3R43213 2012
  940.54'7243515092—dc23
  [B]
                                                          2011036161

∞™ The paper used in this publication meets the minimum requirements
of American National Standard for Information Sciences—Permanence of
Paper for Printed Library Materials, ANSI/NISO Z39.48-1992.

Printed in the United States of America

To those whose fate it was
to leave misery,
suffering, and hunger
for peace and light

CONTENTS

PREFACE

I arrived in New York in September 1951 to study American business methods, to make up for the lost years of World War II when I had been what was called a Freedom Fighter in occupied France.

America was unspoiled. People didn't lock their front doors or their cars. You could travel at night on the subway from the Bronx to Brooklyn fighting only boredom. You could listen to jazz in Harlem, at the Savoy or the Apollo, to Count Basie, Charlie Parker, and many others. Americans were very hospitable and curious about a young Frenchman who spoke English.

I had a wonderful time.

It never occurred to me to tell these Americans that I had been arrested at gunpoint, taken to prison, and beaten, and that I had spent the last year of the war as a convict of sorts in a Nazi concentration camp. They would have been embarrassed.

So many years have gone by, so many generations have come of age, and the world has opened up so much that I can now hope American readers will understand, especially the younger ones for whom World War II is history.

This book is only a personal account, an expression of myself, nothing more. As such, it is rather embarrassing to have people I know nothing about know so much about me.

The translation of the French text into English was a work of dedication, involving in succession two friends of mine, Americans living in Paris, who were so taken by the book that they translated it independently of each other. I would never have been able to do it all by myself. Their contribution was essential, and I am deeply grateful to them.

INTRODUCTION

I was born in Paris in the early twenties. My father had fought the four years of World War I in the trenches and had been wounded five times. When I was still very young he would tell me what it was like and take me occasionally to regimental luncheons at Les Halles to meet his old comrades-in-arms. Whenever we travelled through France he would show me the war memorial that stood in every village, each one with a long list of names. There had been nearly two million dead on the French side. I came to think that war was just a part of becoming an adult and expected to go to war when the time came.

Yet war was unthinkable. People seemed unconcerned. Paris was beautiful and elegant. We had a happy family life. But the pressure was already building. In 1934, during the Nuremberg Congress of the Nazi Party, I heard Herr Hitler on the radio. The voice was harsh, the sentences short. Whenever he stopped speaking, what seemed to be millions of people shouted in unison, "Sieg Heil! Sieg Heil! Sieg Heil!" I was astounded. This voice came from another world. All these young men and women who shouted sounded like fanatics, of one mind, of one heart, united.

In France, after a quiet winter World War II started in earnest in May 1940 and ended rather quickly. The British were back home. The French had one hundred thousand dead and more than two million POWs walking slowly toward Germany. My family had motored down to the South of France ahead of the advancing German armies and settled in the little town of Albi, where I continued my studies.

There was no way to leave France to join the fray, even though my brother Jacques and I could think of nothing else. We were new to this part of France and had no connections, only pocket money. After a few months we met a steely-eyed young man, choosing his words carefully, who said he needed some handguns. Jacques and I happened to know where to get them. At night we broke into a poorly guarded storage place and brought our new friend all the handguns he wanted. We then moved on to bigger things, though still very young, inexperienced, and unprepared. This "Resistance" activity lasted, on and off, for more than two years. It was not spectacular. We were simply gathering military information and passing it on.

Early one morning, May 16th, 1944, there was no knock at the door. But a man barged into the bathroom as I was brushing my teeth and poked a gun in my ribs. That was the end of it. Handcuffs, interrogations, beatings, crammed cells, a cattle car to the Compiègne camp, and then . . .

MY STRIPES
WERE EARNED IN HELL

1

COMPIÈGNE

End of May 1944. In this transit camp, northeast of Paris, are thousands of men just out of the Gestapo prisons who are now free to walk around in the large gathering place between the barracks to meet others and talk. They have much to say. The interrogations, the beatings, the torture are behind them. After what they went through, they do not worry about the future.

Four of us are half-lying on a blanket. We have an old deck of playing cards that we have borrowed.

Sergio di Navarro is a very handsome and elegant Spaniard, about twenty years old. He has the thin mustache of a "caballero," black eyes, and long eyelashes. Ernst Pinxter is a young Dutchman, calm and well mannered. He has blue eyes, and his hair is so light it is almost white. Jacques, my young brother, is rather short, with auburn hair and creased eyes.

All of us were imprisoned together.

Sergio, who is Catalan and claims to have gypsy blood, is good at fortune-telling and has our full attention. At the end he offers to tell us how things will turn out for us in the war.

Sergio shuffles the cards, cuts, and draws one for himself. Ernst draws one, and Jacques draws one. Each time it is a good card. Sergio predicts that he will make it, that Ernst will make it, that Jacques will make it.

Sergio turns to me. I draw a card and place it faceup on the blanket. The change in his expression tells me immediately that it is a very bad card. I raise my hand before he can say it aloud, get up, and leave.

All three died in Nazi camps.

2

NEUENGAMME

THE CATTLE CAR

The train rolls slowly from Compiègne in northern France toward Germany in the stifling June heat. There are a hundred and twenty of us in this cattle car, half-naked, standing most of the time, breathing with difficulty through cracks in the sides. When the train stops at a station or a siding, no more fresh air enters the car, and many of us faint. Bernard Morey is here, Claude Bourdet, and a lot of other French Resistance men.

I lean for a moment against the wall, beside a boy my own age. He says, "It's stupid to have got caught now. The Allies are landing in Normandy."

"How do you know?"

"They parachuted me in a week ago to sabotage communication lines."

We chat for quite a while. When arrested, he was dressed as a farmer with false ID, and the German police did not find out who he really was. He tells me a lot of things he ought to keep to himself. I warn him that if anyone in the car hears our conversation and turns him in, he'll be taken back by the police and tortured until he tells everything he knows.

After three days and two nights of hard travelling, we arrive at Neuengamme, a large concentration camp in the suburbs of Hamburg, the main camp in northwest Germany. We are the second convoy of French inmates to be interned here. Behind the camp square stretch out lines of barracks and a large number of workshops I shall never know about.

SAINT LOUIS

We are in a quarantine barrack for newly arrived inmates. We have been issued summer-weight Polish army field jackets, each with a big orange cross painted on the back, and Polish army pants.

I go out to the courtyard in front of the barrack. A few yards away, a boy who arrived in our convoy, dressed just as I am, is scrubbing out the barrels from which the soup rations were just served. He's singing "Saint Louis Blues" in English, and he knows all the words. For one brief instant, it fills me with joy. I think of Satchmo, the inimitable Louis Armstrong, of the days before this war began, of Saturday night parties in big apartments in the elegant parts of Paris. I think of well-brought-up young boys and girls delicately nibbling little sandwiches between one dance number and the next. That world, which no longer exists, certainly did not prepare me for what I'm living through now.

THE FIRST ORDEALS

In these early days of June 1944, it is snowing in Neuengamme, and the Normandy landing is almost called off because of a major storm.

It is snowing in June.

Because of the enormous number of inmates, the morning and evening roll calls on the camp square last forever. We are counted off row by row, barrack by barrack. Then the total is added up, and we are recounted until the total is absolutely correct. It takes hours. Standing in the snow, I catch a cold. I blow my runny nose in my fingers and rub it on the sleeves of my field jacket until they gleam with snot, as if a colony of snails had walked up my arms, trailing slime.

My cold develops into bronchitis and a sinus infection. My eyes stick together with pus. Every morning in the lavatory, I pry them open with my shirttail dipped in water.

I've also contracted diarrhea, which makes me get up several times each night. I grope my way to the latrine and usually can't find my way back to the bunk I share with another inmate. I finish the night shivering on the cement floor, unable to sleep.

Within a few days, I've become a human rag. A friend has to hold me up at roll call, especially the evening one. At this rate, I'll be dead in a month. I decide to part company with my younger brother Jacques so that he won't become a helpless witness to my death. Jacques was arrested with me. He is determined, resourceful, and in good health. In a moment of confusion, I change barracks.

It's not until we get to Misburg, my next camp, that I will begin to work my way up again, only to topple down and climb back a number of times, but finally to return, still alive, to Le Bourget airport near Paris in June 1945.

THE HANGING

Today we don't go to work, and at first I wonder why. From the courtyard in front of the quarantine barrack, I can see the camp square where inmates are setting up a gallows. We are lined up, barrack by barrack, and marched into place: hundreds, thousands of men at attention, silent, motionless. In the middle, near the gallows, a band made up of inmates begins playing "Beer Barrel Polka," a popular German tune, and other well-known beer-hall songs. We stand at attention for hours.

Finally, the SS officers arrive in polished boots and spotless uniforms. They chat among themselves and smoke expensive cigarettes, handling them with black leather gloves. One of them places a few sheets of paper on a lectern and makes a short statement, which is translated by interpreters into several languages. It turns out that two Russians stole food from a bombed-out house in Hamburg while they were clearing away rubble. They have been sentenced to hang.

The two Russians arrive at last under heavy escort, their hands tied behind their backs. They are very young, calm, and dignified, and they are silent.

They are hanged at the same moment. One falls straight, and the knot breaks his neck. His death is instantaneous. The other, however, falls at an angle. The impact of the knot is broken by his neck muscles, and his body jerks for several minutes. His mouth dribbles and an enormous tongue appears. We see the whites of his eyes. His death is horrible and slow, but finally it's over.

We remain on the square for a while, petrified, until we are finally sent back to our barracks.

The show is over.

In the olden days, the people of Paris went to the gallows of Montfaucon, the site of public executions, just to see that. For the fun of it.

THE FARMER

We are working near the electrified fence. We have formed a human chain, passing two bricks at a time from man to man for hours. At the end, our hands are bleeding and we are exhausted. It is late on a June evening, and the fields, stretching off as far as the eye can see, are magnificent to behold.

A horse-drawn cart comes jolting along the dirt road that runs beside the fence. Standing in the cart is a German farmer, gnarled, with his shirtsleeves rolled up, wide suspenders, and an old shapeless hat on his head, just like any old peasant back home in France. He shouts at his horse to make him go faster and clacks the reins. He's on his way back from his field. He's doing what he must do every day. He sees us, he knows who we are, but he doesn't look at us.

This has been going on for so long. . . .

3

MISBURG

Here in the camp
you ask questions,
but you should not,
as there are no answers.

There are only blows,
and they will break you till you are silent,
and shuffle on with vacant eyes,
staggering under your own weight,
the haunting skeleton of a nightmare.

MISBURG

It is a short trip from Neuengamme to Misburg. When we arrive, the doors of our cattle cars are opened by local police wearing strange, billed caps, their rifles trained on us. They have been told that we are all dangerous terrorists and notorious criminals.

Under heavy guard we are marched through a large petroleum refinery and along a broad canal to a field with a fenced enclosure the size of a soccer field. This is our camp, still being set up. We are not far from the city of Hanover, which we can see in the distance.

VAN HOUTE

July 9 is my birthday. I am twenty-two. We have been at Misburg for two days, and the camp is not yet finished. We sleep under huge tents surrounded by a temporary fence. And now we are watching our first bombing raid on the refinery.

Earlier raids by the Allies have done so much damage that Derag-Neurag, the company that owns the refinery, has put in an order to Neuengamme for concentration camp labor, a thousand men to be added to the Soviets, military and civilian, mostly Russians and Ukrainians, who are treated like animals, French and British POWs, and other categories of workers already here.

I have raised the tent flap and am watching the bombing. I am unafraid, even reckless. Beside me, Van Houte, a comrade from the north of France, is saying his prayers out loud. He believes his final hour has come. I tell him, "You should watch. You won't often see a show like this, not even at the movies."

He turns away and continues to pray, but under his breath.

Antiaircraft guns thunder. Small shell fragments rip into the tent cloth with the sound of popping champagne corks. Hundreds of planes roar overhead. Our eyes burn from the chlorine vapor that the Germans use to camouflage the refinery. A thick cloud of black smoke rises from the refinery.

It is a great sight.

I don't yet know that I am going to spend a full year working at Misburg and that I will end up knowing the village and its refinery as intimately as I know my own neighborhood in Paris.

JOHANN SEBASTIAN BACH

The refinery has been seriously damaged, and there is a considerable amount of urgent repair to be done. We work nonstop, goaded by pitiless foremen, all common German convicts. It is very hot, and we get nothing to drink all day.

I am working on a railway siding that runs through the refinery. The guards are SS men. One of them, a boy about my age, whistles all day long the music of Johann Sebastian Bach, most frequently a concerto for two violins that is a favorite of mine. Though he doesn't know it, we have something in common.

FALLING BRICKS

In July 1944, the refinery is like a beehive populated by thousands of men working to rebuild it. We are near a huge gas storage tank, around which POWs are building a protective wall. They are working fairly high up, on plank scaffoldings, where alternating piles of bricks and buckets of mortar have been set. I am watching a POW who keeps pulling his bucket along the scaffolding as he finishes one section after another. I can see that the pile of bricks at the other end of his plank will surely fall, as soon as he pulls the bucket onto the next plank.

Two German workers, both civilians, are deep in conversation under the scaffolding. The POW works his way along the wall, dragging his bucket toward the end of the plank. The workers below continue talking, and the accident is now inevitable. I watch with intense interest as what has to happen, happens. The bucket slides onto the next plank, the first plank topples, and the bricks start to fall together with the plank, in what seems like slow motion, onto the heads of the two workers, who are still talking away when they are struck squarely on the skull.

The foremen rush up; everybody is screaming. The workers are pulled out of the rubble and laid on the ground. Stretchers are called for, but the two workers are already dead. And I wonder: how could those two not have had an inkling of what was coming? Obviously, their guardian angels were seriously at fault.

But then, so was I, maybe.

HITLER YOUTH

It is now mid-August. The work is very hard, and beatings are frequent. At a certain moment, without having planned it, I find that I'm at the end of a wall. Slowly, I turn the corner and relax for an instant, bracing my chin on the end of my shovel.

A group of children comes along the road on their way home from school, swinging their book bags. One of them catches sight of me and begins to yell: "Mister! Mister! There's one not doing anything!"

And he points at me. I haven't time to get back to my workplace before a hail of blows lands on my shoulders and back. The child looks happy to have done his duty as a patriotic young German, and the others congratulate him. They are all well indoctrinated.

It's my fault, of course. A concentration camp inmate has to pay attention to everything all the time. If he doesn't, he'll be sorry.

THE LIBERATION OF FRANCE

As weeks go by, the French inmates feed their hopes with real news and tall tales. The news comes to us from the few Nazi newspapers in French that are given us by French POWs in the refinery, or it comes from Bouvet, a teacher at Lycée Carnot in Paris, who has avoided letting on that he knows German well and who always works as close as possible to the guards so as to listen to their conversations and report to us. His devotion is remarkable, for it restricts him to the lower class of inmate, while he could easily rise in the concentration camp hierarchy, as foreigners who speak good German are rare.

The tall tales come from everywhere and nowhere. It becomes clear that the French have lost whatever talent they had for accurate oral transmission of information. They are unable to hear and report anything without embellishing or exaggerating it.

It is true that some of us wonder how it can be, as we are told, that all of France has been liberated with the sole exception of its main ports. We wonder also why the Allied troops stopped their advance at the Vosges mountains instead of at the Rhine.

HERMANN'S TRAINING OF CAMP INMATES

Those who knew Hermann, the boss of barrack II, will never forget him. He was a common criminal, about twenty-five, and had been a concentration camp inmate for a long time. It was said that he had committed several murders. He was short but handsome, despite his bulging eyes and a mouth often twisted in fury. He was tough, even sadistic, but also very rigorous and fair. He was a dangerous man, one you should never look in the face. He could beat you with his rubber truncheon to the point of orgasm or exhaustion. I once saw him kill a Greek officer in just that way after a mild infringement of discipline.

He ruled through terror and expressed himself only with shouts and blows, but he often said things we needed to remember. For example:

"Keep your trap shut. Never answer back, never argue, or I'll beat the shit out of you."

"Even if you have no soap or little water, or not enough time, you've got to wash every day, the best you can."

"If you can't get to the sink because of the crowd, wash your face with sand. If the pipes are frozen, wash with snow. Since you have no towel, dry off with your shirt."

"You may think, stupidly, that what I'm saying doesn't matter. But it does: it's a matter of life and death."

"Your past doesn't mean a thing in here. It doesn't exist; it's dead. You have no more name, only a number. I call you by your number. And you have no future, either. You have only the present, and you must give it all your attention. You must handle it the best way you can, minute by minute, hour by hour, day by day. It's the only way you're going to survive."

"You're less than a man now. You're an inmate, a concentration camp inmate. That's all. Try to be the very best inmate you can. That's your only choice."

And that's what I did.

THE SPOON

I suppose I should try to give an idea of the richness of camp expression, especially in Russian.

One evening I am sitting at a table in barrack II, trying to bend my tin spoon back into shape. A friend calls to me, and I turn to respond. When I look back, the spoon is gone. A Russian is sitting on the other side of the table, opposite me. I speak to him in his language: "Comrade Russki, where is my spoon?"

He looks me straight in the eyes: "I don't know nothing about your fuckin' spoon."

"It was on the table."

"I ain't seen no fuckin' spoon."

From experience, I know how to make him tell the truth: "As a Communist to a Communist, tell me, didn't you take my spoon?"

"Shithead Franzusski, stop whining. You want a spoon? Here's a spoon." He tosses my bent spoon on the table, and adds: "You been here long enough, Franzusski asshole, to know anything lying around is common property."

"Russki asshole, I fuck your mother."

"Franzusski asshole, in your condition you couldn't fuck my mother or anybody else."

We go our separate ways, both satisfied.

ALBERT CARRAZ

He's a French barrack mate, a tall, likable fellow. He has difficulty stooping down, lifting concrete blocks, or digging a hole with a pickax. He winces, and tiny drops of sweat form on his forehead. I have to help him out fairly often. He has two bullets in his body and has had no medical treatment.

His problem goes back to the time when he was arrested in Tours and questioned by the Gestapo. Since he did not talk, they arrested his fifteen-year-old daughter and tortured her before his eyes. Albert, whose hands were handcuffed behind his back, edged slowly over to a desk, where one of the Gestapo had left a loaded Mauser. He took the pistol and shot himself twice in the lower back before the Gestapo disarmed him. They threw him on the floor of a cell just as he was, half conscious, losing blood, with his hands manacled. They came back a few days later, and seeing that he was still alive, they removed the handcuffs and gave him a ration of food and water. Later he was moved to Compiègne, a transit camp in the north of France, and then to Neuengamme and Misburg.

When I look at him, I can't believe it. The bullets must have perforated both his kidneys and his intestine, his hip bone may have been broken, yet here he is, working more or less like the rest of us, on his feet through the endless roll calls, living, enduring.

He says, with a smile: "When your hands are manacled behind you, there's no way to shoot yourself in the heart or the head. That's what I would have preferred. Because then I would have been sure that they had cut it out with my daughter. I think, in fact, they did stop, but I can't be certain. I wish I knew how she was. What's become of her?"

He's haunted by the fate of his daughter.

Albert will survive. I'll see him again after the war: tall and thin, with the pale blue eyes of an aviator, wearing an old leather jacket. The Gestapo had sold off everything he had. He got the jacket back only because he spotted it on a passerby in the street. The guy gave it back to him without complaint, a little embarrassed. I can't recall whether his daughter went mad or not.

Albert finished his career at Toussus-le-Noble airfield near Paris, as base commander. He has now rejoined his old comrades after giving to all who knew him an example of dignity, simplicity, and nobility of soul.

THE REALLY TOUGH GUY

In barrack II there is a French jailbird, brought here with the rest of us to make room in French prisons for new arrivals. He is a tough little guy with the inimitable accent of the lower-class Paris suburbs. I find him amusing. I don't understand half of what he says because he speaks underworld slang. I often make him repeat himself so that I can memorize his more colorful expressions. He loves to recount the highlights of his career as a pimp and minor crook, including the finale, when he was arrested on a Paris rooftop in his socks, shoes in hand, because their soles were slippery.

He was on the run from the cops when a hooker turned him in. He swears he'll finish her off if he ever gets back.

When another Frenchman is smoking, he comes along and asks, "How about just one little drag?" He trades his soup and bread for cigarettes with camp inmates who are more prudent and economical than he.

He will die within a few months.

THE CELERY ROOT

It is an afternoon in late September. We have been working at the far end of the refinery, and we are being marched back to camp along the street that runs through Misburg rather than the road that follows the canal.

As so often before, a platoon of tanks arrives with a deafening roar of engines that shakes the windowpanes in nearby houses. Our guards push us to the edge of the street, and I find myself less than a yard away from a van filled with vegetables. They're celery roots. I pick one out mentally, unbutton my jacket and shirt, get up my nerve, and in a flash the celery hops out of the van into my shirt.

I assume a vague, innocent look and carefully rebutton my shirt and jacket. But one of the guards catches my eye. I'm sure he hasn't seen anything. I was very careful, and he was turned away from me. Yet he's looking at me meaningfully, insistently, and I'm beginning to tremble. If he suspects me of larceny and has me searched by the foreman, I'm finished. Even the smallest theft is punishable by death. At last, the guard looks away. The tanks move on. We return to camp, and I taste the raw celery root. I find it awful, so I give it to a friend, Gaston, an old French peasant, the only inmate in the camp to wear a mustache, which he has kept out of sheer stubbornness even though it's against the rules.

PADO AND THE BLACK MARKET IN GASOLINE

The racket was very simple. The refinery was awash in gasoline. All you had to know was which tap to turn. At this time, we were still being served soup from the refinery kitchen at noon, and we also took a short break at about 10:00 a.m., during which the guards ladled out ersatz coffee into our tin bowls, tepid and sugarless, which we drank wherever we happened to be. This coffee came from the camp kitchen, where Russian inmates, accompanied by guards, went to fetch it in big metal canisters. They carried back the canisters in the evening, when we returned from work, swinging them ostentatiously as we passed the camp gate to show that they were quite empty. But, of course, they were full of gasoline.

The gas was stored only God knows where. It was traded to the truck drivers who regularly delivered provisions to Misburg. The racket lasted for a long time, and neither the SS nor Derag-Neurag ever caught on.

It was our comrade Padovani who, though he couldn't speak a single word of German, had "organized" the scam on behalf of the camp boss, the kapo, and a few others. Pado was exceptionally resourceful, to put it mildly. After one bombing raid, he had even "organized" a whole goose, a fat German goose, plucked and roasted to a turn. He shared it with his comrades in barrack II, who never got over it.

Pado was a short, stocky Corsican with jet-black hair, jovial and a bit overweight. Some of us, including Bernard Morey, had known him in the Resistance as Major Armand Philippe. In fact, his name was no more Padovani than it was Armand or Philippe, and he wasn't even a Corsican, but none of that matters. The Germans, all the Germans at Misburg, called him "Fatso," with a certain grudging respect.

And he deserved it.

HANS

Hans was a German common-law criminal. On the front of his convict jacket was sewn a downward-pointing triangle of green cloth to show that he was dangerous. Yet he was a fairly ordinary-looking fellow, with sallow, flabby skin, globular eyes, and soft features. He looked at us with an indefinable expression, a combination of envy, hatred, and despair. I came to understand that look later on, when I learned that he was suffering from a serious heart ailment and had only a few months left to live.

He was in charge of a work crew, and often, when we were at the refinery, he would sit down and hold his head in his hands. He trembled and perspired and made desperate efforts to regain his composure, but he seldom succeeded. I saw him cry several times. When his fits were over, he took it out on us for his own temporary weakness, as of course, we usually had taken advantage of it by not working. He would hit hard and accurately, as only a German can strike a defenseless man.

One day, I was stupid enough to talk back to him, and I got a first-class beating. After that, he loathed me. He kept me on in his crew for the sheer pleasure of sticking me with all the hardest chores, until one day he tired of tormenting me and allowed me to transfer out.

Life went on and I had almost forgotten about him when some weeks later I went to the infirmary to visit a sick comrade. On the next bunk, there was Hans, his face bathed in sweat, breathing with difficulty, his eyes staring nowhere. He was dying. I approached quietly and watched him for a long time, without moving, without smiling. He turned his head, and his eyes met mine. In those eyes were all the rage and hatred of a man reduced to silence and impotence. He tried to breathe regularly, but he couldn't. He knew that I knew he was going to die. He would have wanted to kill me. But I could look at him that way only because he could no longer touch me. I came back the next day and his bunk was empty. He had died during the night.

BRONTOSIL

Christian Caillé was a French medical student, a camp inmate who was in charge of the infirmary because he spoke good German. At that time he had a supply of dark red pills, a German medicine called Brontosil, a sort of aspirin.

One evening, when inmates lined up outside the infirmary for sick call, he gave two of the pills to a Frenchman. The Russian who was next in line complained of diarrhea, and Caillé, who had no medicine except the Brontosil, sent him away empty-handed.

At roll call the next morning, the Russian is at his place, looking awful and embarrassed. He is as red as a brick. His condition is noticed. There is a conference between the guard checking off the ranks and the barrack bosses. Caillé is called over to consult. Someone rubs the Russian's face vigorously with a wet rag, but the red color remains.

Caillé goes to the infirmary and returns with the explanation. Overnight, the Russian had broken into the infirmary and swallowed half the bottle of Brontosil. Everybody burst out laughing, especially the guards and the camp trustees, but that evening the Russian gets twenty-five strokes on the back to teach him not to steal.

The camp being what it was, I doubt the lesson did him any good.

THE PNEUMATIC DRILL

One morning our work crew marches through the refinery and ends up in front of a concrete wall that had been shattered by bombs, leaving big chunks still connected by iron rods. Russian workers set about severing the rods with a blowtorch. The concrete blocks fall off one after another. They fall any which way. Not a single one lands flat. A pneumatic drill is produced and turned on. It falls to me to use it. I crawl up on the nearest pile of blocks, dragging the drill after me. I aim it at the middle of a block and lean into it with all my strength, gripping the handles for dear life.

For a few seconds, the drill grinds against the concrete without much result, and then it slips. I manage to hold onto it, and a second later I am lying on the ground, practically on top of the drill. Blows rain down on me, together with insults from the foreman. I climb back up the sloping pile of blocks, lugging the heavy tool. A few seconds later, I fall again, like the first time. The foreman is really furious, and he strikes me so hard and for so long that I'm on the point of blacking out. The civilian refinery official who is in charge of the demolition project tells him to stop and pick a stronger man to handle the drill.

I am soon back among my comrades, picking up fragments of concrete that others cart away on wheelbarrows. I breathe a little easier. My back, my shoulders, and my head are aching. My hands are badly scratched, and I am still shaking from head to toe from the vibrations of that cursed machine. I work through the morning to the sound of the powerful drill.

The inmate who replaces me is a stocky Russian, obviously less awkward than I am. He finds cracks in the blocks as well as places to brace his feet. He works cleverly and he succeeds. Concrete pieces fall one after another. The work goes ahead. The foreman is pleased. At ten o'clock, we get our ersatz coffee. The Russian sits down beside me and looks at me out of the corner of his eye.

"I eat the same as you," he says. "I sleep the same, I live the same. So tell me: how is it that I can do this work, and not you?"

I don't reply. The Russian stands up, ready to go back to work, strong and erect. He then answers his own question: "Because you're a degenerate capitalist and I'm a socialist, that's why."

I didn't dare contradict him. Even now, when I hear a pneumatic drill in the streets of Paris, I walk the other way.

THE POKER GAME

One day when it's raining cats and dogs, our guard marches us to shelter in what appears to be an empty shed. Inside, however, we find a group of British POWs playing a cutthroat game of poker, with piles of worthless "prisoners' marks" on the table in front of each of them.

Their guard is sitting in a corner. Now and then, one of the British disdainfully tosses him a cigarette to keep him quiet. Our presence disturbs them, and they show it. So our guard marches us rapidly out again, anxious to spare us a sight he clearly regards as indecent.

FIGEAC

A good number of the Frenchmen at Misburg were from Figeac, a town in the Southwest of France. After the Résistance pulled off an operation in the vicinity, all the local men were summoned to have their identity cards checked at city hall, and those who were imprudent enough to comply ended up on the road to Compiègne, Neuengamme, and finally, Misburg.

There were the local shopkeepers, the butcher, the cafe owner, and the tobacconist, who had known each other forever and who formed a homogeneous group. There was also a young man I liked a lot, Etoc. He was a talented painter, a complete innocent, and he bore his misfortune with courage and dignity. He never returned. He left behind him a wife, a little girl named Prune, and a few canvases.

BERNARD MOREY

He wandered through life with the face of an archangel, deep blue eyes, and a very slow voice. He spoke German well and, as a result, managed to win a certain amount of respect from the camp trustees and the guards, especially when he told them he owned a large pork processing plant.

One evening, when the soup was being dished out by Mishka, Hermann's Russian boyfriend and the orderly for barrack II, Bernard can't find his tin bowl. Someone has stolen it. Mishka tells Bernard to hold out his jacket and pours a big ladle of soup onto it. The liquid passes straight through the dirty cloth, leaving only a handful of vegetables.

Bernard is utterly downhearted when he tells me the story. I start hunting around the barrack. I see a bowl momentarily set aside by its owner. I "borrow" it nimbly and carry it back to Bernard, saying, "Look, I found your bowl."

He is delighted, but then a Russian turns up, insults him, and snatches the bowl out of his hands, even though Bernard tries to hang onto it. So I had to steal him another one and, on top of that, appease his conscience with a lie. Bernard couldn't stand the smallest dishonesty.

VLADIMIR

Vladimir was an ensign in the Soviet navy. He came from Nikolaev, on the shore of the Black Sea. We were together in a ruined building, pretending to work, and Vladimir was drawing long puffs on his last cigarette, its ash end bright red and pointed like a pencil.

He addresses me in his own language: "Hey Franzusski, have a puff with me."

I react like a "petit bourgeois," as my Communist friends would say: "Oh, no, Vladimir, it's your only one. Smoke it all yourself."

Vladimir shakes his head and says, "We're comrades, brothers in misery. If you don't smoke, I don't smoke."

Whereupon he tosses the cigarette down and stubs it out with his heel.

Ah, the Slavic soul!

THE CAMP BOSS

He was a small nervous man, not a bad fellow really. He wore a wide, dark blue beret that made him stand out from the others, and he carried a short rubber truncheon, which didn't hurt very much, even when he struck with all his might. He was a criminal, and I saw him more as a confidence man or a sex pervert than as a murderer. In order to have been put in charge of the Misburg camp, he must have been an inmate for a long time and proved his mettle to the SS in one post after another, as in any other organization. Above all else, he wanted to keep his job and avoid trouble. As inmates in his concentration camp he wanted men who were not ill and who could work hard.

He was a master of "organization." It was he, along with Padovani, who "organized" the gasoline racket over the summer. When the bombing raids in the Hanover area became much more frequent, he also "organized" civilian soup for us. Thanks to his "organizing" skills, he lived comfortably in a small room at the back of barrack I, with clean sheets and towels and even soap. After he left, I found an almost-empty tin of Nivea skin cream in there. I am sure he got plenty to eat every day, as did all the common criminals who ran our camp. Once he even "organized" some schnapps and showed up on the camp square one evening completely drunk, unable to speak a sensible word and racked with hiccups, to the delight of the inmates. The SS commander simply sent him back to his room to sleep it off.

The camp boss intended to stay alive no matter what. In his room I also found a cone-shaped, one-man concrete bomb shelter, which he must have had built with concrete stolen from the refinery and which he must have used during the numerous air raids over Misburg. I was to see him for the last time at Bergen-Belsen, in a special area reserved for trustees, surrounded by other concentration camp figures, neat and clean, waiting for the end.

I never knew his name.

THE SANDWICH

There are a dozen of us in a work crew marching through the refinery. Our guard is Winter, a fat, jovial sergeant-major and also Misburg's official executioner. Killing a camp inmate doesn't bother him, but he never kills without a reason.

It is raining hard, and Winter has ordered us to take shelter in a hut used by the German refinery workers. There are a table and two benches, and clothing hung on pegs along the wall. There is also food on the table.

Gazing innocently about the room, a French inmate whose name I've since forgotten slides a fat, well-filled sandwich across the table and into his shirt. He strolls away from the table and goes into a corner. I am not the only one to have noticed his act. A Belgian inmate has seen it, too. The Belgian walks over to the Frenchman. They talk for a minute in low voices, and then both begin to chew ferociously. In an instant, there's nothing left.

Suddenly the refinery workers show up. They're not at all happy to find us in their shed. They sit down at the table and start to eat. One of them looks around for his sandwich, but in vain. Suspecting what has happened, he starts screaming at Winter, who screams right back. Then Winter calms down, looks us over, questions us. It doesn't take him long to identify the two guilty parties. They turn pale and tremble. He marches them outside, draws his pistol, and coldly shoots them dead. We return to camp carrying the two bodies, which we put down in the middle of the camp square.

That evening we are given a speech by the SS commandant on the theft of German property and its consequences. The speech is translated into several languages by our interpreter, Edouard, a small, harmless-looking man, though he was a former agent of the Comintern, the international espionage arm of the Soviet Communist Party.

The Frenchman who was killed was a bartender in Deauville and the Belgian a barber in Tournai. I never found out whether the German workman regretted having opened his fat mouth.

"NIGHT AND FOG"

One day, a new German criminal arrives here from Neuengamme, a young dark-haired fellow with a downward-pointing black cloth triangle sewn on his jacket and two large black crosses painted on the back. Two broad bands have been shaved across the top of his head to form another crude cross, marking him as confined to camp and not allowed to work in the refinery. One might ask why he has been sent to

Misburg, but it really doesn't matter. He must be particularly dangerous because everyone fears him, from the camp boss to the barrack bosses and the foremen. He belongs to a class of inmates called "night and fog," NN in German, because they have been sentenced to long-term solitary confinement.

One day he disappears. Everyone goes wild. There's a special roll call, a search of all the barracks, the infirmary, the outbuildings, the entire camp. He's nowhere to be found. Time goes by. The SS commander is in a towering rage, and the guards are panicky. We inmates, standing in the camp square, make ourselves as inconspicuous as possible, wondering how this all will end.

But the NN guy finally turns up by himself. He had managed to sneak into the septic tank by prying up some floorboards and had spent hours hanging from an underground beam for no other reason than to irritate the shit out of everyone, as it were. He's hauled before the SS commander and beaten until he's unconscious, but he never cries out a single time. He is sent back to Neuengamme, where, so we hear, the SS hanged him. I have to think he didn't give a damn.

In the course of his short existence, he had gone too far out to ever return among his fellow human beings.

EUROPE

The life of the thousand concentration camp inmates at Misburg would have made a fascinating study for a sociologist. First, there was the mythological dimension, the camp gods, the SS guards who had the power of life and death over everyone. When speaking to them, we stood at attention precisely three paces away, cap in hand and eyes down. To look them in the face would have been a serious insult to their dignity, meriting instant punishment.

The demigods, or trustees, who made up the camp hierarchy were long-time German inmates who had survived years in the camps. They were opponents of the Nazi regime or, as at Misburg, common-law criminals. They ran the system for the SS and profited from it: the camp boss, the barrack bosses, the kapo (short for "comrade policeman"), the foremen, and others, too, cooks, dishwashers, orderlies, electricians, and so on. Their work was easier than that of the ordinary inmates. More important, they were better housed, warmer, better fed, cleaner. But they continued to serve out their sentences, nonetheless, and remained at the mercy of the SS.

Finally came the concentration-camp underclass, including me, dispensable men, all in the same uniform, with the same shoes, the same bunks, the same rations of soup and bread. We lived on a footing of almost absolute equality, which nevertheless concealed some minor inequalities among us.

There were those whose soup was served from the bottom of the barrel and those whose soup was skimmed from the surface, where it was thinner and less nourishing. Some worked in small crews, always with the same crewmates, doing specialized work, and others were assigned to big heavy-duty crews with tasks such as repairing the railway, where one man was interchangeable with another. There were those who managed to earn a bit of extra bread or soup, like the Russians who took turns standing guard over the piss barrel, or like our Communist barber, Mimile, whom the Germans called "the Jew," although they treated him the same as everyone else. There were those who smoked all their cigarettes and those who hoarded those precious commodities and auctioned them off at night behind barrack II. Some even kept them in their shirts for days on end, waiting for the price to rise. The SS and the camp hierarchy made the members of this underclass work until they dropped dead and punished them as they saw fit, without discussion or delay.

These men came from the many European countries occupied by the Germans. There were many Soviets, Poles, Frenchmen, Belgians, Dutch, Italians and Spanish refugees living in France who had been turned over to the Germans by the Vichy government, veterans who had fought in the Spanish Civil War against Franco, some Greeks, mainly officers, calm and quiet Norwegians who kept to themselves; and even some Buryats from Central Asia, tough little fellows with coppery skin and slanted eyes, and some I've forgotten, no doubt, after forty-five years.

All these men lived, worked, and suffered together regardless of nationality or class. A teacher from Lycée Carnot in Paris slept side by side with a tram conductor from Kiev. A workman from the Ferrari plant in Modena lent his cup to a Norwegian herring fisherman. Among themselves, they spoke "kitchen German," grammarless and always in the familiar "du" form: "Me happy that you do. You not happy, you say." They understood one another's words and feelings. National differences, though still present, faded to insignificance compared with what united them.

There were men of every political stripe, but with a very large number of patriots. There were some skeptics, for whom the left and the right are complementary, who believed that democratic societies do not progress in a straight line. There were a few men of deep faith, Catholic priests or convinced Communists, who put themselves at the service of their fellow men, gave as much of themselves as they possibly could, and died of their efforts in the end.

It was Europe from the Atlantic to the Urals, and even beyond, a Europe that has never existed anywhere but in the Nazi concentration camps.

THE BUM

I'm talking with Bernard Morey. He asks me, "What would you like to do after the war? If you ever get home?"

I think it over. I have to admit I never think about it. I live day by day, hour by hour, minute by minute, watching everything around me.

"I can see becoming a bum. I'm sure there are lots of places in Paris where you can sleep without being disturbed. All you have to do is settle in discreetly. As for food, you can always buy day-old bread from the baker, as much as you want."

"What!" says Bernard. "You'd be a beggar, you wouldn't work, you wouldn't even try to recover, to build a new life?"

"I don't know. I would need a lot of strength. I think that for a while I'll be satisfied with existing as a bum, as anything you like, but free."

"In that case, you shouldn't stay in Paris. What will your relatives think, your family, your friends, if they see you in that condition? You should come to my town, Cuiseaux. I'll find you a place to live, and you can eat all you want from my family's canning factory."

"You're right, Bernard, and I appreciate your generous offer. But you have to admit one thing. Being a bum would be a real step up from what we are now."

THE BREAK

Since July, the refinery has not been bombed very often, and now, at the end of October, the work has become much less strenuous. With a questionable sense of economy, Derag-Neurag has stopped serving soup at lunchtime. The company also informs the SS organization that it has no further use for half the camp population, that is to say five hundred of us. The camp boss, assisted by the barrack bosses, makes a selection on the camp square. They pick out the inmates who won't give them trouble, who speak some German, and who work hard. They have no use for shirkers. They reject those who are totally exhausted, including my friend Bernard Morey, those who are too old or too young, and those who can't understand orders, primarily Frenchmen, Italians, and Belgians.

They keep the Germans, Russians, Ukrainians, and Poles, who are obviously better adapted to conditions in the camp than we are. Hermann keeps Jean Mattéoli and me in his barrack. Sad and fearful, we watch our comrades leave to return to Neuengamme. But what can we do? Life in concentration camps is a daily lottery. You can never know in advance whether your number will come up.

THE GASOLINE STORAGE TANK

Twelve inmates are crouching, sitting, or leaning against a low brick wall a few yards away from a huge gasoline storage tank. One of us is smoking. He is a young Russian, a product of Stalin's short-lived "free love" policy. He grew up without parents, in the streets. He's a robber, a liar, and he has no fear. He's smoking tobacco from old butts wrapped in newsprint, an incredibly bitter blend. He holds the "cigarette" cradled in the palm of his hand. The smoke rises into his sleeve. When he exhales, he lowers his head and blows the smoke down his shirt. It's a pretty good system, but it doesn't quite disperse the smell of tobacco smoke, and the guard sitting and facing us is getting jumpy. He aims his weapon at us, pointing the barrel at one after the other, but he can't identify the guilty one. We stare back stupidly, pretending we don't understand his shouting. Finally he tires of the game and orders us up and back to work.

The storage tank did not explode after all.

MARTIN

Martin Kurz was a German "political" inmate, like me and most of the French in Misburg. According to him, all he had ever done wrong was to make a few imprudent remarks when his ship was in port. They arrested him eight months later, on his return from a trip to Narvik, in Norway. Martin had been a merchant seaman for many years. He had travelled a lot and knew all the great ports of the world. We spoke English together, even English slang, and we spent hours on end discussing the size of the waves near Sydney, Australia, and the incredible beauty of Rio de Janeiro and Honolulu. During those brief periods, we forgot the concentration camp universe. He talked to me about the United States, where I had never been, described the little restaurants on Fisherman's Wharf in San Francisco, and told me about the San Quentin penitentiary, where he had done time for running marijuana out of Mexico. To hear him tell it, San Quentin was something like the Ritz Hotel with the climate of the Riviera thrown in.

Everybody in the camp called him Willy. He didn't know why and he didn't care. Physically, he looked like an old clown without makeup, with big, sad eyes, in a striped uniform much too big for him, with a constant drip at the end of his nose, though he conscientiously wiped it with his sleeve. He wasn't a foreman because he didn't care for responsibility or discipline. But he had carved himself a modest little niche in the camp, which provided him with extra soup to trade for cigarettes.

One day like almost every other day, a day with a "major alert," we are together in one of the barracks because there isn't enough space for all the inmates in the two covered trenches that serve as bomb shelters. It is November 26, 1944. The Misburg camp is about a hundred yards from the refinery, which turns crude oil into airplane gasoline and many other products that are essential to the war effort. Inside the barrack, we sit in silence, listening seriously, intently, to the noise outside.

Suddenly, Martin jogs my elbow and says, "Listen, sonny boy. You don't have a cigarette, do you?"

"Yes."

"Do we smoke it?"

"No."

"Listen."

"No."

Time passes, and suddenly we hear the airplanes very distinctly. At the same moment, the German 105-mm anti-aircraft guns open fire, and everyone rushes to the door to avoid getting caught inside the barrack.

Martin says nervously, "Now is the time to smoke, or never."

So we hurriedly smoke my last cigarette, alternating puffs. The guns are still firing, and the planes are directly overhead.

I say to Martin, "Don't worry, nothing's going to happen." At that very instant, the first bomb load falls and explodes some distance away. The impact knocks us down, but we get up. Martin passes me the cigarette. I take a final puff and go out, leaving him leaning against the barrack's brick chimney.

The American planes glitter high in the sky, but they are easy to identify. They're B-17 Flying Fortresses. They arrive in perfect formation, circle, and unload their bombs right over the refinery into the artificial chlorine smoke while the antiaircraft batteries continue to fire.

This lasts several minutes. Soon more bomber formations appear, but—this I don't understand—they don't circle. They keep coming and coming, and the lead plane releases a signal flare directly above us. I race to the trench, running like mad, and hurl myself into the hollow entrance. I curl up with my head in my hands. And the bombs fall all around us. I get up the best I can and see the fence breached in several places, the barrack where I had been standing in ruins, and three huge craters in the camp. And then it starts all over again: once, twice, three times. I can no longer think. I'm petrified. My head is in the dust, and it makes me cough.

Then nothing, no sound. Whistles start to blow, men start to scream, and everyone starts running toward the fence, to the barracks, to the bombed-out trench. There are dead and seriously wounded men everywhere. More Flying Fortresses appear, and everyone hits the dust again. The bombs fall rather close to us. Minutes pass. A plume of thick black smoke rises above the refinery and blots out the sun. At last the all-clear siren blows, everything quiets down, and everyone hurries to his own barrack. I didn't see Martin again until late the following evening. He was in bed in the infirmary, completely hidden under the covers, with only a lock of hair showing. He sticks his head out from under there, the head of a good old lovable bastard, and says: "Well, sonny boy, I thought nothing was going to happen!"

He got away with a broken collarbone and a lot of bruises.

THE FACTORY SMOKESTACK

The factory smokestack at the Derag-Neurag refinery was tall, round, and made of brick, like every factory smokestack anywhere, including in the north of France and the Paris suburbs, with this one difference: since November 26 it had a jagged hole, which almost cut it in two. In its graceful fall to the ground, a 100 percent American bomb had punched straight through it, opening a small seven-foot hole where it entered and a huge seventy-foot hole where it exited. Depending on where I was working, I could see the sky through the two holes.

The smokestack, like a grand old duchess, lasted to the end of the war without anyone daring to repair her.

THE BRICK WALL

One night, the refinery is bombed once again, and we spend four hours in the covered trenches that run along the sides of the camp square. We are in total darkness, squeezed in together like subway passengers at rush hour, feeling the earth tremble around us at every explosion. By now, we've grown used to it. We can even recognize the different types of bombers. This night, it is not the usual Halifaxes or Lancasters, but Mosquitoes, which, like their insect namesakes, make diving attacks at precise targets.

In the morning, we discover the extent of damage as we proceed through the refinery in search of the civilian foreman we were working under yesterday. There he is, in his heavy boots and cap and thick leather jacket. He's standing next to what was once a fuel tank but is now a mass of twisted and blackened metal plates. The brick wall we were building around the tank has melted in the extreme heat. All that is left of it is a little brown mound with tiny pinstripes in it, like a banker's suit. The stripes are what remains of the mortar between the bricks. You'd have to see it to believe it.

THE CIVILIANS

From the camp we could see the road and the village of Misburg. We could even make out something of the life of its inhabitants. All the men from sixteen to sixty had been drafted, and those who remained were women, children, and old people, together with the foremen and technicians from the refinery, many of whom had already fought in the war and had returned wounded. The women took their husbands' places at work in the fields around the camp, loading the harvest into little carts pulled by wolfhounds.

Hanover is on a direct line from London to Berlin. So since November there had been a bomb alert every day. Night and day, Allied planes filled the sky with their droning roar. Often, they were on their way to bomb another city, but the civilians in Misburg still rushed to their shelters whenever the planes passed overhead. I watched them on the road, pushing baby carriages filled with their most precious belongings, heading toward the big concrete shelter at the crossroads. After a false alarm or a real raid they returned home by the same road. Often, they make the round-trip several times in a single day and several more times the next night, always with the same courage, the same tenacity, the same discipline.

During the daytime, the Americans practiced what they called "carpet bombing," saturating the target and its immediate surroundings with bombs.

Many civilian houses, especially those near the refinery, were damaged or destroyed. The owners repaired or rebuilt them the best they could.

And life went on.

THE CRACKING TOWER

The refinery got its crude petroleum from wells in the area. This crude was distilled, or "cracked," in a tall, round tower fitted out with platforms at various levels, iron stairs, and complicated pipes. Since November 26, this tower boasted yet another decoration: a truck hanging stupidly by its rear axle from one of the platforms. A bomb had exploded right under its chassis and sent it twenty yards into the air.

Unfortunately, it came to rest directly above one of the refinery's internal roads, and no one liked passing underneath it. The civilians were free to make a detour, and our guards always stepped carefully out of range. But we, formed up in ranks, had to pass directly underneath it, our buttocks tight with fear. One day some workmen dislodged it, and it fell to the ground without hurting anyone.

THE FREE WORKER

At the end of November, some new inmates are transferred here from Neuengamme. Among them is a Frenchman who is in good physical shape and speaks good German. One evening, after the soup, he tells me his story. Back in Paris, he signed a work contract, received the usual bonus offered by the Nazis to foreign workers, and came freely to Germany, where he was assigned to a factory near Berlin. He found a German girlfriend, and through her he met a couple of dubious characters. He quit his job and moved to Berlin. With his new friends he lived off the black market and then joined a gang that stole suitcases in railroad stations.

He tells me, "It's easy work when there are three of you. Lots of people put down their bags when they buy a paper or a magazine. They glance away from their luggage for a few seconds. That's when you have to make your move, fast. If needed, your two accomplices cover your escape by knocking papers off the rack or leaning over to tie their shoes. If worst comes to worst, they may even pretend to start a fight. Most of the time, though, that isn't necessary. Ten or twenty seconds is all you need to disappear if you know the station. We used to sell the suitcases, without even opening them, to a fence who was a 'specialist.' He paid us according to size. From his point of view, it was a lottery. Sometimes there were clothes or sausages, sometimes really valuable things.

"You know, the people in railroad stations these days are almost all refugees. All they have with them is what they managed to save from the bombs. We were very careful, and when there were suspicious-looking characters hanging around, we held back. But the police planned their raid well. One day, a guy who put down his valise and started leafing seriously through *Signal* magazine really did look like a refugee. His bag must have been full of stones or books. Anyhow, it was very heavy. I was having trouble lifting it, and he was already all over me. My two pals started running, but they got caught at the main exit.

"So here I am. The end of the good life! I did live well, and I had a great time. In a way, I was even a kind of hero, because I was doing something against the Germans."

I reply, "Unfortunately, you can't award yourself a medal. Someone else has to decide you're a hero, and, frankly, I doubt if they will. But then, you never know."

He says: "Yes, you never know. But we have plenty of time. What we have to think about is getting out of here alive and not feetfirst. And, to tell you the truth, it doesn't look that easy."

No, not easy at all.

THE TRENCH

We are at the refinery, not far from the road, doing a particularly tough job. We have to dig a deep and narrow trench for a new pipe, but the gray Hanover mud is sticking to our spades. A group of French POWs comes whistling down the road and watches us slave away, urged on by screams and blows from the foreman as he paces up and down the length of the trench. One of the POWs calls out: "Hang on, you guys. We're settling scores for you: We're fucking their wives." I didn't believe what he was saying, and I may have been wrong, but he made me laugh. This infuriated the foreman, who didn't understand a word he said.

THE BURNING HOUSE

One autumn afternoon, we're marching back to camp along the street that runs through the village, when a bombing raid begins. Our small crew of twelve inmates and a guard starts to hurry. We see a burning house. It has taken a direct hit from an incendiary bomb. A German civilian dashes out and appeals to the guard for help in saving his furniture. The guard picks me out for the job, along with another inmate. I go into the house, walk down a hallway and straight into a kitchen. I open the refrigerator, take out a bottle of beer, and open it, using the door hinge. I begin to drink from the bottle as fast as I can. Beer spills on my chin and my jacket. The fire roars through the house. Even the kitchen ceiling is in flames. But I go on drinking. Once the bottle is empty, I grope my way through the smoke, find a door, and go out the back way, coughing heavily. The house collapses. The guard decides not to hang around any longer, and we set off toward the camp.

I have remembered that beer for a very long time. Few beers I have ever drunk gave me so much pleasure.

THE SECRETARY

One of the refinery's administrative buildings has been demolished by a bomb. We are on the road that runs beside the building, clearing away the rubble and tossing bricks onto the smoking mound, which is all that remains of the building. A big black car drives up, the kind used by refinery executives. A fat German civilian gets out, followed by a fairly pretty young girl. They stand there looking at the mound of bricks and then begin to climb it. We find this funny. The sight of the young girl tickles us, and we begin to make jokes at her expense, make obscene remarks, and whistle. The fat German pretends not to notice, but the girl blushes. They're looking for records, file cabinets or something like that, but there are no such things to be found on the smoking pile. They come back down, get into their car, and drive away. They probably had to find an office somewhere else.

THE CRUSHED FINGER

I am working on the scrap-iron crew. We are collecting twisted railings, steel plates, and other metallic debris from the bombing and dumping it into a railway car. But the freight car is high on the embankment, and it takes a superhuman effort to lift and load the heavier pieces of scrap. Once, being in the lead, since I see no other way of doing it, I place my hand on the edge of the wagon to steady myself while the others push the metal up and off my shoulder. And then, blam! An enormous steel plate crashes down on the middle finger of my left hand. It hurts like hell, but I go on working anyway. That evening, I look at my finger. It's not a pretty sight. The next day it's even worse. It hurts so much that I can't use my left hand. My finger is swollen to double its normal size. I go to the infirmary and see Caillé, who tells me, "Your finger is crushed. There's nothing I can do for you. Go back to work."

He adds: "In any event, there's nothing to worry about. Either you'll survive or you won't. Whichever the case, the problem will be resolved."

Some difficult days and nights follow. The pain is so intense that I spend the day with my teeth clenched on a little block of wood I picked up off the ground. I can't sleep. My lymph glands are swollen. I can't think about anything but my own mounting pain, a pain which I keep to myself, turning inward, second by second, minute by minute, hour by hour. I go on working with only my right hand the best I can until the day when a guard notices my awkwardness. He calls me over, and I stand to attention. He says, "Show me your hand." I show him my right hand. He says, "No, the other one." I hold out my left hand, wrapped in dirty rags. He says, "Take off those rags." I unwind them. He studies the enormously swollen white finger for a long time, shaking his head. Then he speaks to the other guard, asks him to take over the whole crew for a while, and motions me to follow him.

Off we march to the infirmary reserved for the German workers and their families, which has been set up in a concrete bunker.

We go down a short flight of stairs and take our place in the waiting room, side by side, with the guard's rifle resting between his legs. Everyone stares at us. I'm scrawny, run down, and repulsively filthy. I'm wearing the same uniform I had on when I came to Misburg five months ago, so thickly covered in muck that the stripes are scarcely visible.

The children in the waiting room hide their faces in their mothers' skirts. The grown-ups whisper. They have never seen a concentration camp inmate so close. I don't know what they've been told about us, but they seem to be afraid of me. Pretty young nurses in spotless white uniforms pass through from time to time. At last, it's my turn. I go into an office alone and sit down, and a fat doctor inspects my finger. I try to explain to him that he mustn't cut it off, but he doesn't appear to be paying attention. He opens a cabinet, takes out a pair of sharp little scissors, inserts them under my fingernail, and with a short, sharp gesture rips off the nail. Then he applies some disinfectant and makes a nice, clean dressing. I go out and return with the guard to the work detail.

So I never went back to that infirmary nor to the camp infirmary. I took no medicine, and I didn't change the dressing, despite the fact that as time went on, it became disgusting and finally fell off by itself. I went on working, living. The pain decreased, things became normal again, and I forgot all about it.

WRITING HOME

There are French POWs working at the refinery, always the same men. We cross their path often, and sometimes we manage to exchange a few words. They have been here since 1940 and have become real manic depressives. One day, they call out: "Cheer up, it won't be long now!" The next day, they're distant and silent.

One of them, Gualbert Lienard, allows me to use his monthly postcard to send news to my family. It's November 19. I write: "I'm working with my cousin. It's not too hard, but we're anxious to see the end of it." The card goes to England and is rerouted, finally reaching my parents' home in Paris. I still don't know why it took that roundabout route.

At about the same time, another POW, Jean Degat, gives me another card. This one reaches Paris by way of Basel, Switzerland. On this one, I write: "I think of you with love and courage. . . . I will come out of here strong and proud, worthy to live happily in a free world."

God bless those two men whose simple kindness brought my family so much relief.

SHOES

The shoes we were issued when we left Neuengamme have wooden soles and cloth uppers. By November, they are held together miraculously by pieces of wire. At a certain point, we receive an allotment of new shoes from Neuengamme. But such is the insane logic of the concentration camps that there are only two hundred pairs while there are five hundred of us, all with shoes that are totally worn out, except, of course, those of the camp hierarchy.

Hermann hands out the shoes allocated to barrack II. He is very fair about it. He carefully examines the shoes that each inmate brings to be replaced. But the problem has no solution. During the next few nights, there occurs the most extensive stealing of low-quality shoes since the dawn of history. As for me, I use my new shoes as a pillow. I knot the laces around my neck, so that I am sure of being awakened by a strangling sensation at the slightest effort to steal them.

Ever since the war, I have always slept on a hard pillow.

HEISE

Heise is an honest and kindly man. He's a supervisor at the refinery who does all he can to lighten the lot of the inmates assigned to work for him.

Last night was one long bombing raid, and we got almost no sleep. Now it's Sunday, and we ought to have the day off. But ten of us have been sent to Heise's house to repair the roof, which was partly blown away by a bomb. This isn't the first time it's happened, and Heise knows exactly what needs to be done. So it is that Jean Mattéoli and I, along with a few others, learn how to repair a roof, a skill which, I must admit, we shall have little use for in later life. We spend the day there, happy to be of service to this man, until the time finally comes to put away our tools and inspect our work.

We should now go straight back to camp. But Heise has a word with the guard, after which he invites us into the house. Imagine a dozen concentration camp inmates, all disgustingly filthy, sitting down to table with a German and feasting on rabbit with noodles served by his wife. At the start, I feel very embarrassed, but then, like the others, I begin gulping down the food, which rapidly disappears. Heise hands out cigarettes and, very simply and naturally, starts a conversation going. The atmosphere in this German home is extraordinary, with the kind husband, the welcoming wife, and a little girl who sits on Jean's lap and asks him to sing a French song.

I can't believe it. I feel like I've rejoined the human race. But the guard is becoming impatient. We thank our hosts, depart, and march off to the camp. That was one Sunday I have never forgotten.

Heise is long since dead. His wife is still alive. I've been meaning for years to go visit her with Jean and to bring her a brace of fine French rabbits. But I've never got around to it.

LICE

At the end of November, a new group of inmates arrives from the East. A few weeks later, I'm covered with pimples. I can't stop scratching. I go to see Caillé and tell him, "I can't stand the camp food anymore. Look."

I take off my shirt. Caillé cannot believe that I am so naive. He asks whether I'm trying to make fun of him. At length, he says, "You have lice, just like a number of your mates, and there's no way you can get rid of them. Your clothes will be infested with lice, the bedcovers will be infested with them, the camp will be infested with them. And there's nothing you can do about it."

He is right.

For months afterward, like the other inmates, like so many poor people back home in the olden days, I'm totally louse ridden. I carry on a sneaky war with them, but it's lost before it begins. I often catch them on my shirt collar or coming out of my sleeves. But mostly in the evening I crush the louse eggs secreted in the seams of the shirt and drawers that I've been wearing since I got to Misburg. My technique is to squash them against the red-hot stovepipe that heats the barrack. The result is a series of sizzles that is music to the ears. Unfortunately, no matter how many I destroy, I always miss enough of them so that the beasts can go on multiplying. I'm covered with scores, even hundreds, of bites. And like my campmates, I can't help scratching and scratching again, sometimes until I'm actually bleeding. And this had to happen to me, a man who had already got scabies in the prison in Bordeaux!

Lenin is supposed to have said, "Either socialism will defeat lice or the lice will defeat socialism." I don't know whether Russian lice ever heard of either Lenin or socialism, but I do know that they were completely at home in Hitler's Germany.

THE POTATOES

With winter coming on and the Allied bombing raids continuing, it has become harder for the SS authorities to provide us with hot soup in the evening. The soup has been replaced by a handful of cold potatoes, doled out from a barrel that a Russian inmate rolls along from table to table. Everyone passes his bowl to the man at the head of the table, who holds it out to the Russian orderly. Hermann watches, his truncheon in his hand. All the rations must be equal. There is to be no discrimination.

One evening, in the midst of this delicate and critical operation, a potato falls out of the Russian's sleeve.

Hermann swoops down on him and grabs the sleeve. Out falls another potato, a second, a third, a fourth. Flabbergasted, we realize that the Russian has been stealing potatoes from under our noses, even though we never let him out of our sight. Hermann holds onto the Russian's sleeve. He begins to shout and work himself up into a rage: "So, you filthy bastard, how could you do that? How could you steal from your mates? You're garbage! You're shit! You wait: I'm going to fix you for good!"

He hauls back to hit the Russian with all his might, but his victim slides to the floor and begins to scream with pain before he's even hit. You should see Hermann's face, his eyes popping out, completely baffled. He pulls himself together quickly and starts the beating, but inefficiently. The Russian is too low, and he keeps rolling around. Hermann goes on pounding him, the Russian keeps on yelling and then slithers under a wooden cot. Hermann chases him, screams, flails away. The scuffle moves all around the barrack floor until finally an exhausted Hermann comes to his senses and returns to complete the distribution of potatoes. The men, all standing up by now, were not sure they would get anything to eat tonight.

Next day at morning roll call, the Russian's face is bruised and swollen, his eyes black, but he's alive, calm and standing up straight, surrounded by his Russian comrades, who are plainly prepared to defend him from the other inmates. After that, Hermann never hit him again. When their paths crossed, he stared incredulously and turned his eyes away. The Russian had got away with it for the time being.

THE TOBACCO PLUG

One day, by one of those odd turns of Nazi acquisitiveness in occupied Europe, we each receive a package of chewing tobacco. I must say I can't recall what country it came from.

We haven't been able to brush our teeth since we arrived in Germany, so I decide to chew some as a matter of hygiene.

Jean Mattéoli sees me with a bulge in my jaw and says, "You look like an old sailor."

I explain why I am chewing.

He answers, "You're right, and I'm going to try it. Only very sparingly. I wouldn't want to get the habit."

I add, "I'd like to point out that this stuff makes you salivate. You have to spit every five minutes."

Jean observes, "At least here we won't have to spit into the wind as if we were on a ship. All we need do is avoid spitting on the other guys' shoes."

And so it goes for about two weeks, until the supply runs out.

THE ITALIAN RAILROAD MAN

At Misburg, as elsewhere in the Nazi concentration camp system, every escape attempt was punishable by death. And yet a certain number of attempts did occur. On these occasions, we were lined up by fives after work on the camp square, where a machine gun was aimed at us while nearly all the guards set off to search the countryside for the escapee. Their orders were to search the area for a half-mile around. In the German army, orders are orders, and sometimes we spent the entire evening and part of the night standing at attention until the first guards began to straggle back exhausted and the SS commander allowed us to return to the barracks.

We are eating our soup one day when we hear shouting and whistles blowing. Hermann and Mishka drive us outside with their truncheons and make us line up on the camp square. Once the ranks are formed, Winter arrives, leading an Italian inmate who escaped about ten days ago. He's dressed in a German railway porter's uniform, complete with black pants with a wide red stripe down the sides. He smiles and nods to his friends. He seems happy to see us again and to pass us, as it were, in review. He even looks amused. He walks slowly all the way around the camp square, ending up before the SS commander, who addresses a few words to us. Then Winter draws his pistol and shoots the Italian in the head.

Such is the rule.

THE WATCH

We are heading back to camp under the usual guard, marching down the middle of the street that runs through Misburg, when a tank column arrives with an enormous racket. The guards push us over to the sidewalk, where we're tightly packed together. I find myself just a yard away from a civilian, a neat-looking fellow with a coat, a scarf, a hat, gloves, and well-polished shoes.

I ask, in German, "What time is it, please?"

He looks at me, removes a glove, opens his coat and jacket, and takes from his vest pocket a large gold watch and chain. He looks at the watch and says, "It's exactly a quarter past four."

"Thank you ever so much," I reply.

He tips his hat and says, "My pleasure, sir."

And watches as the tanks roll on.

MAXIM

Maxim is a Soviet schoolteacher from a small Ukrainian town, and he amuses the French because all he knows about French literature is Alexandre Dumas and Émile Zola. Physically, he is extremely dirty, which is saying a lot, considering the competition, very much like a hobo. He lives bundled up in rags and sheets of paper held together by wires under his uniform.

A group of us is working on a bombed-out railway spur, saving any undamaged ties. Among others there is Jean Gambier, a lawyer from Rouen, a marvelously suave character. He was sent to Misburg from Kiel, where he had been digging up unexploded bombs for the German navy at a rate of one a day. It is delicate work and so dangerous that the Germans call it "the walk to heaven."

Gambier belonged to a resistance network directed by Colonel Buckmaster of the British intelligence service. It channeled downed Allied airmen all the way to Spain. He was arrested six months earlier while dining at a well-known restaurant in the Place des Ternes in Paris. He saw the Gestapo moving toward his table with their hands on their pistols. So rather than try to hide among the other customers and perhaps cause casualties in the restaurant, he rose and walked directly toward them, waving gaily at the other diners with both hands, which was more honorable than putting them on his head. Most people in the restaurant never even looked up.

Jean doesn't eat much for breakfast. He keeps his slice of bread in his shirt to eat at noon, which is what he has just now done, eking out the meal with a Norwegian herring he got hold of God knows where. All that remains of this herring is the head, the backbone, and the tail, mixed up with some other assorted refuse on the railroad tracks. Suddenly, we see Maxim's hand, rummaging between Jean's feet, grabbing the fishy skeleton, which he devours in a gulp.

Jean watches this with astonishment and asks in Russian, "Was it good?"

"Yes, very good."

"Well, so much the better," observed Jean, with wonderment.

Work starts again.

One way to lift a railway tie is to sink the head of a pick into one end with a hefty blow and then lever it up hard while another worker slips a crowbar underneath the tie to tip it over on its side. So doing, we uncover a nest of field mice, squeaking in surprise at the sudden sunlight.

Jean turns to Maxim and says, "Eat, very good for you."

Maxim doesn't hesitate a moment. He catches a live field mouse, holds it by its legs, bites into the stomach and chews painstakingly, as the blood pours down his chin. Jean can't believe his eyes. He turns away and throws up his lunch. He starts cursing himself for having made the stupid suggestion and cursing Maxim for having taken it literally. I burst out laughing. And the work goes on.

RIO DE JANEIRO

We are in the refinery, standing in the driving rain, shivering, drenched from head to toe, trying to escape the worst of the downpour by huddling up against a half-demolished brick wall. Then all of a sudden my mind is a thousand miles away from this cold and watery universe.

Jean Mattéoli jogs my elbow and asks, "What are you smiling about?"

"I was just thinking that, at this very moment, in Rio de Janeiro or somewhere else, there's a group of boys and girls our age who are piling into a convertible. They're going to picnic on the beach and dance in the moonlight."

"And you envy them?"

"And how!"

At which point the foreman begins to yell and we go back to work in the rain.

THE PISS BARREL

Soup for supper, combined with our weak bladders, makes us get up several times every night. To cut down on nocturnal wandering in the camp, Hermann has put near the barrack door a metal barrel with two stout handles, which the inmates relentlessly fill up, one after another. It is guarded by a young Ukrainian wrapped in a blanket and perched on a nearby stool. When the barrel is almost full, he sends the last two pissers to empty it into the septic tank at the other end of the camp. When we have the urge, we listen carefully to the sound of each stream falling into the barrel: a low sound when it is almost empty, a high one when it is almost full, the purpose being to avoid getting assigned to the emptying detail.

One night, I can't hold out any longer, so despite the high-pitched sound, I go along and piss. And I am assigned along with another fellow to empty the barrel. I'm in my shirt and drawers, barefoot, and I protest the order, asking to be allowed to go back and put on my shoes. No, says the Ukrainian, who knows full well I'll not come back. He threatens to call Hermann, so I take one of the handles in both hands, the other inmate takes the other handle, and the Ukrainian opens the door for us. Here I am, barefoot in the snow in the middle of a freezing night, staggering down the length of the camp square, which is lit up like daylight by searchlights on the fence, and carrying a heavy vat of piss.

I look at the gorgeous sky, at the bright, twinkling stars, and think, "If only my father could see me now!"

CIVILIAN SOUP

One night, the barrack is suddenly lit up. Hermann and Mishka chase us outside with curses and swinging truncheons. We form ranks in front of a soup truck in the middle of the camp square. This soup is not in the wooden barrels we are used to, the ones that are rolled along the ground, but rather in heatproof metal casks. It's civilian soup. To those who rush forward Hermann yells that there will be plenty for everybody. When the time comes, it turns out to be thick indeed, rich in meat and potatoes, a wonder. The truck contains so much of it that we take seconds and thirds, even fourth helpings, lining up for each new serving.

Later on, we learn that every time there is a bombing raid on a German city, the authorities cut off the water and gas mains in the area to avoid flooding and explosions. There are vast underground soup kitchens in the area, which distribute unlimited free soup for the first few days following each raid. But many civilians, when their homes are completely destroyed, simply leave and take refuge in villages or on farms. So there's soup left over that nobody knows what to do with. Our camp boss has done a magnificent job of "organizing" a deal with the soup-truck drivers against a share of our cigarette rations. This is the result. The SS commander did not bother to get up for the occasion, but he has no doubt left orders to let the party proceed.

THE RUNS

We are standing lined up by fives at morning roll call, and I have a worrisome problem. I have diarrhea, and the roll call just won't end. The work details will be put together immediately afterward, and I won't have time to get to the latrine at the other end of the camp.

What I feared happens. We're marching to the factory five abreast, hemmed in by guards wearing so many layers of clothing they look almost ridiculous.

The cold is sharp, minus five or ten degrees Fahrenheit, but the wind that so often sweeps over the Hanoverian plain has dropped. Our wooden clogs echo on the packed snow. The sky is dark gray, and the big red sun is so pale you can look straight into it. Our condensed breath makes a light mist above the marching column. The picture is unreal and magnificent, but I'm in no condition to enjoy it. It's getting harder and harder to keep my sphincter tight. I'm counting the minutes till the time I can pull down my pants. Finally, I can't hold off any longer and, without turning my eyes, I address the guard who is marching along beside us: "Latrine, please, sir."

He starts yelling. I can understand little of what he says, except that he doesn't intend to stop the whole column of marching men just for me.

So what has to happen, happens. It comes rushing out with a loud noise, fills my drawers, and with each step I take flies off the legs of my pants. I go on marching, robotlike, with a vacant expression on my face. But the guard heard the noise, and now he can smell the shit. He looks at me with a mixture of disdain and disgust and makes this remarkable comment:

"These Frenchmen really are a bunch of pigs! Makes you wonder how they were brought up!"

A PAIR OF GLOVES

We're working in the refinery, near a gas tank that has been destroyed by a bomb. As usual, a Russian crew is chopping up metal plates with a blowtorch, and we are carrying the scrap to a nearby railcar. The metal fragments are sharp, and my hands are covered in blood. All of a sudden I notice a civilian from the village standing at a bus stop about twenty yards away, watching us. From where he's standing, the guard can't see me, and I am overwhelmed with an urge to express my rage and suffering to someone, anyone. I start shouting at the civilian: "Why are you watching us that way? We're not animals! Leave us alone!"

He probably doesn't understand French, but he can see my hands, which I raised while I was talking. Glancing right and left, he walks toward me, removes his gloves, and drops them at my feet. Then he sets off at a run toward the village. I pick up the gloves, marvelous wool-lined leather gloves, and I slip them on with delight, even as I watch the civilian disappear. I smile and think about the man's courage, the risk he has run just to alleviate my sorry condition.

I am proud of him.

THE CHRISTMAS TREE

A fine, well-decorated fir tree has been set up in the middle of the camp square. Each of us is given a cupful of slightly sweet brown beer, and the SS commander, his words interpreted by Edouard, asks each of the different national groups to sing. The Germans go first, the camp bosses, the kapo, the barrack bosses, and the cooks and foremen. They sing loud and clear and with obvious enjoyment "O Tannenbaum" and "Lili Marlene." The other inmates listen, standing in a big circle. Then come the Russians, who spontaneously join their magnificent voices in a series of Slavic melodies so beautiful and sad they make you weep.

Finally, the Russian chorus breaks up, and Edouard calls on the French, who consult and reconsult with one another until the SS commander starts to show his growing impatience, and they strike up "La Madelon." After a few bars, many of us don't know the lyrics, while others go on singing anyhow. The result is a discordant racket. Laughing, the SS commander tells us to stop and go back to our barracks.

It has not been our day.

CHRISTMAS MASS

Despite everything, a few of us have managed to have some contact with the surrounding German population. The priest from the Misburg church goes to see the SS commander and asks that Father Leroy be permitted to celebrate Christmas mass in the camp. Permission is granted, and the priest brings in all that Father Leroy will need. The news spreads among the Catholic inmates, and our dear priest starts confessing all those who want to take Communion. But there are so many of them that he will never finish in time, and he is brokenhearted.

I reassure him in my own way. "What counts, father, is that they repent their sins. If you ask them all to make an act of contrition, then you can then give them all absolution, as a group."

Which is just what he does, to the great spiritual satisfaction of those for whom that mass and that Communion will remain forever the high point of their lives at Misburg. There is a small problem, to be sure, when some of the young Soviets in barrack IV, where the mass is to take place, have to be chased away. They have no notion of religion and are just curious about the proceedings.

It is hardly the time to try to convert them.

THE BATTLE OF BASTOGNE

We can judge the progress of the last, desperate German offensive by the behavior of the Germans in the camp. The common German criminals who make up the camp hierarchy are ecstatic. They learn what is happening from the guards, and the news spreads like wildfire. You would think that they want the concentration camps, of which, after all, they are victims too, to last as long as possible.

I hear the boss of barrack I tell Hermann: "We have a tank column heading for Brussels and another on the way to Paris. We're going to drive the British and Americans back into the sea!"

At last their final, desperate dream of glory and conquest dies, and normality returns. As for us, we now know what a German victory might mean here.

THE INFIRMARY

By early December, more than a hundred inmates have died from exhaustion or hunger, not to mention the widespread diarrhea due to chronic malnutrition, which causes food to run through the body, or the monstrous abscesses that begin with an infected flea bite and end up covering half an arm or leg, producing a glassful of pus in a day. The rest of us have reached the limit of our strength. The infirmary has been enlarged, with space taken from barrack III. But to get in, you have to wait your turn. Caillé simply cannot take in everyone.

On December 28, the temperature is somewhere between minus five and minus ten degrees Fahrenheit, and I stagger off to work in a surrealistic setting. Snow on the ground, a dark gray sky, red smudges of brick walls, black splotches of burned-out metal girders. The guard, who is wearing so many clothes he looks like a medicine ball, huddles near a campfire, which we feed with pieces of wood picked up in the refinery. We line up in Indian file with picks and shovels to clear the snow and dig up the frozen ground.

I stick my shovel into the snow, turn up my jacket collar, pull the sleeves down over my balled fists, and shiver. I shiver, with my head hunched down, just as I shivered night and day through the long autumn weeks when it rained and I could never completely dry off. I shiver, using up precious calories, because I don't eat enough, because my clothes aren't warm enough. I shiver from head to toe for hours, doing nothing, watching my comrades, the sun, the sky. Trying to endure.

And I faint. When I come to, I find myself near the campfire, where my mates have carried me. The guard signals me to stay where I am. That night, I am admitted to the infirmary. At last!

THIS ABOVE ALL

The British POWs I meet in the refinery are nice to me because I can speak English. Sometimes they slip me bread or cigarettes. One day, one of them gives me a book, which I conceal under my shirt and then hide in my straw mattress. I keep it in the hope that someday I will find a chance to read it. That chance finally comes when I am admitted to the infirmary, completely exhausted, unable to stand up or do any work at all.

I settle into my bunk under three blankets and open *This Above All*, noticing that the cover is stamped as property of the British POW camp. It's a recent book, a pacifist novel that has gotten by the German censors. The hero is in London when war breaks out. Then he goes to Colorado to buy raw materials and ends up at a big ranch with a swimming pool, where he falls in love with a girl who rides horseback all day.

Suddenly, I am out of Misburg. I've escaped. But the book ends, and here I am, back in my filth and misery and hunger. I throw the book into the toilet.

NEW YEAR'S EVE

In spite of the fleas, I spend a few happy days in the infirmary. The patients don't have to get up during air raids, so the siren that has just sounded doesn't bother me. I've already turned over and dozed off when the bombs start raining down. The building shakes. I'm thrown out of bed. The shock wave has flung the window wide open, and the cold air is rushing in. I go to the window to close it, and I can see the flashes of the exploding bombs, one after the other. The night sky is alive with flares, tracer bullets, and the explosion of antiaircraft shells, all this with tremendous noise. Each time a bomb explodes, a gust of wind hits me in the face. I close the window, hoping the panes will take the pressure. They do. I go back to bed and to sleep. I didn't hear the all-clear siren. I must have been very tired.

GILBERT

Gilbert comes from the eastern part of France. He has been at Misburg since the beginning. He's a solid, serious lad, and I like him. He has lost one eye. He is by training a repairer of stained-glass windows.

It's January 1945, and I'm still in the infirmary, resting, out of the cold, on my back most of the time, amusing myself by hunting for fleas. I take a few steps from my bed and discover behind the open door a bowl filled with slices of bread. A few seconds later the bread is under my shirt and then in my stomach.

No one sees anything.

Thereupon, Gilbert arrives, coming from the toilet, and complains: "I've got the runs, so I can't eat soup. I swap my soup ration for bread. I only eat just what I need to survive, no more. I had my bowl full of bread, and I was such an asshole I hid it behind the door when I went to shit. And now it's disappeared!"

I look at him for a moment and finally decide to say nothing.

"You're right, old man, you were an asshole, and you're paying for it."

He walks off, shaking his head. He dies a few days later. I think of him often, especially since where he is now he knows I stole his bread.

MY LETTER TO JACQUES

At Christmas they distribute a special kind of postcard that can be used only by inmates within the concentration camp system. My brother Jacques left Neuengamme for Sachsenhausen a few days before I left for Misburg. I take one of the cards. With the help of a friend, I painstakingly write out my message in German and hand it to Hermann. A month goes by. One evening, Hermann calls me by number: "34595." He looks embarrassed and hands me back my postcard. Inked across it in large black letters is the word "DECEASED."

I go off in a corner to cry. But I can't. I don't want to believe it. Jacques, who is only twenty, who has never been sick. Jacques, who is so tough, so strong, so clever. Jacques, whom I purposely left so as not to be a burden to him. How can he be dead when I'm still alive?

I learned later that it was true. He died on December 31, 1944, at 7:00 p.m., during a bombing raid. He was in the infirmary, sheltered, giving English lessons to German physicians for use after the war. He caught tubercular meningitis and died in a fever. He did not suffer. He was cremated at the camp, and his ashes were scattered in the fields to fertilize the German soil.

May he rest in peace.

A CRUSHED FOOT

Caillé kicks me out of the infirmary on January 11 so that he can give my bed to someone else. I return to work, but the Germans know the end is near, and they don't push us too hard. I haven't much strength, and I can scarcely stand up. I've become a living ghost. My eyes stare into space, I don't speak, I don't listen. All my gestures have become infinitely slow. In this condition I somehow hang on until February 1, scarcely working at all. That day I clumsily put my left foot in the way of a falling metal plate from one of the gas tanks. The skin breaks, the foot immediately swells up, and that evening I'm back in the infirmary, brought there by a guard in spite of Caillé's opposition. He doesn't want to see any more of me.

Once again, I'm in bed under three blankets, and I sleep almost all the time. I hobble around the infirmary on crutches. I look at my foot, swollen up with an edema produced by malnutrition. The wound is still open. It's a chilling sight, and I still don't know which bones are broken. I don't want to end up an invalid. So, after a few days, I start getting up at night and hobbling about silently in the dark. With considerable difficulty I manage to exercise my foot, and things seem to be improving. But one night Caillé turns on the lights and catches me. The next day, February 14, he sends me back to work. It's not quite so cold, and this time I have a bit of my strength back. I limp, and my foot is a good excuse for not working, so I do as little as possible. The wound heals. I'm going to make it.

GOEBBELS'S ARTICLE

March 1945. The snow is melting, the weather is fair. Fighter planes fight their battles over our heads, and we hear the staccato spurts of their machine guns. Jean Mattéoli shows me an article in a Nazi newspaper in which Goebbels describes the war between the Germans, the British, and the Americans as a "war between brothers." He calls for an anti-Bolshevik coalition to halt the advance of Soviet troops and prevent Europe from becoming Communist.

Mattéoli says, "A little late to think of that, isn't it?"

Wonderful Jean. The soul of dignity and quiet courage. Even here in the camp, he's earned everyone's respect.

I don't know what's to become of us. At worst, the war will go on between the Anglos and the Soviets, and we may well find ourselves in Siberia for the duration. We'll just have to adapt and survive. I now feel that I have become part of the concentration camp world, and I refuse to consider that I may one day live any other way. Besides, we've been abandoned. No one has raised a voice in our defense. The Allies have very good intelligence. It is not possible that they are unaware of what is going on in the Nazi concentration camps, all the more so since the camps have existed for more than ten years. They were first used to incarcerate the German opposition: Communists, Social Democrats, Protestants, and others. There was even a British white paper on the subject, which was also published in French and which I read before the war. There were even a few French concentration camp inmates whose families bought them out, paying for their freedom with gold. They were released in a Swiss town on the German border. These former inmates described what they lived through. No one believed them.

I feel I have to mention the Holy Catholic and Apostolic Roman Church and its Italian pope, who was the nuncio in Berlin and a great admirer of the Führer before being elected pope by the College of Cardinals. The Vatican had no need for a special intelligence service to know all about the Nazi concentration camp system and the extermination of Jews and Gypsies in Eastern Europe. Its priests lived and served even in the tiniest villages of Poland and Germany.

The Church said nothing and did nothing.

DEPARTURE FOR BELSEN

The muffled thunder of artillery rolls across the camp night and day. The Allies are rumored to have reached Osnabrück, sixty miles west of us.

Roll call on March 31 brings a speech from the SS commandant: "You are being transferred to a camp where you won't have to work and where you will simply wait for the Allied troops to arrive. Those who can walk will go on foot. Those who can't will remain here until further orders." Our interpreter, Edouard, translates this into several languages, ending with his traditional phrase: "Well, Frenchmen, did you understand?"

Too many inmates fall into the group that wants to stay at Misburg, and that upsets Edouard, who adds: "Those who can walk but still want to stay will get twenty-five blows with a truncheon." Rather quickly, the ranks of those wishing to stay thin out. There remain only about twenty of us who really are too weak and would rather die here than on the road. The others form into a column on the camp square, flanked by guards. The camp gates open. The camp boss, who has been taken unawares by these developments, wants to go back and collect a few things from his room, but his request is answered by a tremendous punch in the face from one of the guards. The boss lines up with the others. The column sets off.

It is at this moment that I realize concentration camp discipline is no longer of any importance. The inhumane but necessary discipline, the German discipline that allowed us to survive up to this point, no longer has any justification.

THE LEFT BEHIND

Our comrades march off down the road, and we stay with Winter as our only guard. We wait, standing in the square and awaiting the worst. But Winter, who knows me by now, says to me: "A truck will be coming to pick you up tomorrow morning to take you to join the others. Meantime, go to barrack I, all of you, and stay there."

He turns his back on us and leaves immediately. For the first time we enter the trustees' barrack. We discover their comfortable quarters as well as the private room of the camp boss.

We are wondering. Some of us think Winter is lying, that he is going to execute us. We discuss this for a long time. It is now getting late, and we need to eat. Despite Winter's order, we sneak into the kitchen and the next-door storeroom. We find a barrel of marinated fish from Norway, which some Greek inmates roll back to barrack I before opening it. I find some potatoes and cook them on the barrack stove. I share them with Jean Gambier, another of the "left-behind ones."

During the evening, Winter shows up. We stand up hastily. He sees the fish barrel and says, "It was lucky for you I didn't see you sneaking out! Now, close the doors and windows! And lights out!"

I go to bed. For a long while, half-asleep, I hear the Greeks chatting among themselves in the dark, eating and calling one another by name: "Apollo! Economidis!" In the morning, we open the windows and the door.

The Greeks are lying near the half-empty barrel of fish, dead, like idiots, of indigestion. The concentration camp diet has weakened their bodies to the point where they couldn't take the extra food.

THE TRUCK

During the morning, a truck arrives. We climb onto the truck bed, along with Winter, and watch the countryside roll by. For almost a year we've seen nothing but Misburg and the refinery, so the change of scenery is pleasant. Winter is calm and leaves us alone. His murderous zeal seems to have vanished like a spell. We're heading north, and we are travelling through a forest when the deafening roar of American bombers swells up and Winter orders the driver to stop. The planes are B-25 Liberators. They fly very low, diagonally, ten or fifteen abreast. There are hundreds and hundreds of them, and it takes them a long time to fly by. They can fly so low because they have nothing to fear anymore.

We start up again and drive for a while. Then the truck slows down, and we detect in the air a smell we have come to know well, the smell of corpses. The truck stops. Winter jumps out. The rest of us slide down, and we find ourselves facing a large barbed-wire gate. SS guards open it and chase us inside, yelling loudly. As night falls, we enter Bergen-Belsen.

4

BERGEN-BELSEN

At daybreak I saw
For the first time
The hundreds and hundreds of bodies,
Naked
Stacked up around
In the camp.

Some, their eyes glazed,
Seemed to be grinning at me
From their hollowed cheeks.

A faraway voice floated in the mist:
"Do not be afraid, my friend,
This is your home now.
Soon you will join us
As they all have,
And be at peace."

Starved and bruised,
I shrugged
And looked to the sky,
But there was no way
To escape the horror
That would last until
The madman died.

ARRIVAL AT BELSEN

The gate closes behind us, but not a single SS guard enters with us. We are surrounded by a group of young Soviets who were obviously expecting us, as they immediately start searching us and taking everything we've brought from Misburg, mainly our potatoes and our fish. The camp is ill lit, and you can barely make out the huts. The Soviets point out to us one with an open door, and we go in. It is appalling. There is nothing and no one in here, no barrack boss, no bunks, no pallets—nothing but a handful of pale beings stretched out on the bare floor. They don't even seem to notice us. The floor is covered with human waste and scraps of clothing.

I explore a bit and finally come up with a garden spade, which I bring back to the hut. We use it to shovel up some of the filth and clear a space where we can try to sleep. But I see that one of my comrades from Misburg has been knocked down and is being beaten by the Soviets, who are trying to take his rubber boots. I lift the shovel and start swinging at random. The Russkies run off, some of them with bloody heads. We dig away all the muck we can, more or less clearing an area a couple of yards square. We go to sleep practically on top of one another. I sleep sitting with my back to the wall, the spade near at hand.

In the early morning at first light, I go looking for the toilets. They exist all right, but they are full of corpses, stacked up to the ceiling. All the dead are skeletal. I relieve myself, my eyes riveted on what were once men, men who laughed and ran and loved. In the middle of the pile is a pair of eyes that are not glassy like the others. One of the skeletons is looking back at me. He's been lying here, with the others piled on top of him, for God knows how long. But he is not yet dead.

I hasten to rejoin my comrades, and we go outside. Things are just the same there. There are corpses everywhere. There's a pile behind the hut, another here, another there. We even see two men, too weak to stand up, crawling along on all fours and occasionally exchanging a few words. I set out to see whether there isn't, somewhere in the camp, somebody distributing something to eat.

THE CAMP

I contemplate the scene. Bergen-Belsen is a big camp, with scores of huts, surrounded by a thick forest that starts just a few yard past the thick barbed-wire fence and stretches off into the distance. It's in a kind of natural clearing, far from any civilian settlement. The site was well chosen for starving large numbers of people to death. I recall that when we arrived at Neuengamme, the SS officers ordered the old, the sick, and the feeble to fall out so that they could be sent to a camp where they would not have to work. They no doubt came here, for it's not far away from Neuengamme. They all must have died long ago.

A main road starts at the gate and runs straight through the camp, dividing it in two. The men's barracks seem to be mostly on the left. They are built of wood, with cracked paint, dilapidated and dirty. There are some large buildings on the right, one of them apparently the camp kitchen. There seems to be no organization here, just gangs of Soviets who exercise de facto control of the camp. Some inmates don't even have striped uniforms. They're wearing the same civilian clothes they had on when they were arrested. Later I learn that they are Jews from Central Europe.

THE WOMEN'S CAMP

Along the main camp road, there's an SS guard standing alongside a large handcart. A couple of inmates wait nearby. The guard yells at me to join the detail, and we set off, dragging the empty cart. The guard opens a gate in a barbed-wire fence, and we enter the women's camp. The path is winding, and the huts are set back from it among young trees. At various points along the edge of the path are piles of naked female corpses piled up like logs, just as in the men's camp. We load some in the cart. When it is full, we return to the central road and head for the far end of the camp, some of us pushing, some pulling our heavy load.

The guard tells us to stop, and we maneuver the cart to the rim of a large pit, some thirty feet deep, which is already half full of corpses tossed in any old way. There is already a considerable number of them. By now, I don't even notice the smell of death that hangs everywhere. Once the cart is empty, we return to the women's camp and fill it up again. I make the same trip, back and forth, all day long, without stopping, without drinking or eating anything.

At a certain point, as we approach, a group of women emerges from one of the huts carrying a young girl's body wrapped in a blanket. They weep as they hand it over to us with elaborate care. They try to tell us how wonderful the dead girl was. We exchange a few words in German. To cheer them up a little, I tell them that I am an American and that the Allied troops will be arriving very soon. Their faces light up and they slip me some bread, which I hide under my shirt. I have often thought that I may have carried the body of Anne Frank to her grave.

A MORNING AT BERGEN-BELSEN

I'm outside, with Father Leroy.

"I won't tell the others," he says, "but I can say this to you. I just don't understand how God allows such horrors to go on, how He can look on and not intervene."

"But, father," I reply, "you forget that there have always been such horrors and that God has always stood by. I don't want to offend you, but you certainly recall that the Spaniards killed millions of Indians in Latin America and completely destroyed their ancient civilizations in the very name of Jesus Christ."

"Yes, it's probably true. But they thought they were doing the right thing. They thought they were converting pagans, saving their souls."

"Everyone always thinks he's doing the right thing. By the way, I wonder whether the German soldiers still have the old motto 'Gott mit uns'—God with us—engraved on their belt buckles, like the Kaiser's soldiers did. I haven't looked. And besides, father, you know there's the Kingdom of God and the kingdom of man, and that they're not the same kingdom at all."

"I don't understand you," Father Leroy says. "You find all this normal. But I'm shocked that the Nazis, who are Europeans and should be civilized people after all, can behave the way they do here and elsewhere."

"We were in the Resistance, father, don't forget that. We were fighting them. Remember what we called ourselves: 'soldiers without uniforms.' They had every right to shoot us on the spot. Yet now, after a whole year in the camps, after everything they've made us go through, we're still standing up. Not very strong, I admit, but standing up. When I think of all our comrades who have already died, I guess we shouldn't complain too much. Besides: complain to whom, who cares? The only thing to do is shut up and go on as long as we can, hoping we can make it to the end. That's all."

PAUL'S DEATH

That evening, I return to the men's camp and share my bread with Jean Gambier, Sergio de Navarro, and Ernst Pinxter. I've been with the last two from way back, since well before Compiègne, before Neuengamme and Misburg. Sergio is a splendid fellow. I met him when they marched us out of prison and packed us into a freight car at Bordeaux. He is a Spaniard. Sergio's father was mayor of Barcelona during the Spanish civil war and took his family across the border when Barcelona fell to Franco. Sergio was arrested in Toulouse one night when he was bicycling down the landing strip of a German air base, God knows why. He was dressed like a zoot-suiter: long jacket, tight trousers, white socks, and triple-soled shoes. He loved life, girls, and jazz. He was always good humored. Now he's just a shadow of his former self.

Ernst is a young Dutchman from a prominent family who was arrested trying to cross the border between France and Spain to join Allied forces. He's intelligent, cultivated, and refined. He has a huge, sloping brow that is impressive.

Night falls, and the Soviets herd us all toward a hut with triple-decker bunks all the way around the walls. There's a narrow corridor in the middle, leading to the door. They lock us up in absolute darkness. I'm stretched out near Jean, Sergio, and Ernst. We hear Paul groaning. Paul was with us at Misburg and before that in the port city of Kiel, where the German navy had him digging up unexploded Allied bombs. He's an engineer, so one day when the German bomb squad was late, he disarmed a bomb all by himself, thereby frightening hell out of everyone on the scene. Now, though, Paul is at the end of his rope. He's dying at the other end of the hut. He groans and calls for help, but there's nothing we can do for him. Here we are, four of his closest friends, stretched out in the dark, silent, open eyed, listening to him and absolutely powerless. Paul must have disturbed his neighbors. They haul him out of his bunk and throw him down in the corridor, where he goes on moaning, only more softly. In the morning, he's dead. His clothes are stripped off and he is thrown onto a pile with a few others who, unlike him, died in silence.

After the war, I attended a memorial service for Paul in Lyon. I shook hands with his parents, his relatives, his friends, his colleagues. I did not tell them about the way he died.

THE STOLEN RUTABAGAS

The camp appears to be out of the line of battle, for the sound of gunfire is infrequent and far away. I have no idea how the Allied troops are doing, and I'm beginning to worry. Since I arrived, no soup or bread has been handed out in the men's camp. That's why I go along every morning with the body-cart crew to the women's camp, where there's sometimes a scrap of bread to be had. But after a few days I can't take it anymore. If I go on doing this, I won't be able to look at a woman for the rest of my life without thinking of all those corpses.

So I stay in the men's camp with my friends from Misburg. From where we are, we can see a pile of rutabagas about six feet high on the other side of two rows of barbed wire. Between the wires there's a kind of corridor, along which an SS guard marches back and forth.

We count the seconds out loud, Jean Gambier, Sergio, Ernst, and I, in order to determine the exact time between the guard's rounds, and we decide to steal some rutabagas. We find an iron bar about three feet long, twist one end, and sharpen it. We find two jackets that still have buttons on them and fashion them into sacks, and we rip up the clothes of dead inmates to make rags. Each of us is assigned a task. Sergio and Ernst, who are very weak, will stay near the barbed wire and fill the sacks. Jean will pull open the wires, using the rags to protect his hands, and I, taking the greatest risk, will go through the fence into the corridor, where I will spear the rutabagas with the iron bar and throw them to my comrades. We pull it off once, then twice. Then other inmates start to do the same, jumping into the corridor in a disorderly and disorganized way.

The guard, who for some unknown reason has turned around unexpectedly, screams at us, raises his rifle, cocks it, and takes aim. There are three of us in the corridor, ten yards away from him. I see the tiny black hole at the end of the rifle barrel pointing at me. I'm paralyzed. The shot goes off. The guy next to me falls. Somehow, I scramble back through the wire and mingle with my friends. I'm no longer in danger, but I'm stunned by the aftereffects of fear. I'm flat on the ground, unable to move or speak or think, pissing in my pants. It takes me a good fifteen minutes to recover, with my friends gathered around and making fun of me the whole time. Then we eat. We have enough rutabagas to hold out for a week.

THE CHAPLAIN DIES

Rutabagas are truly awful to eat, but they are all we have. Jean Gambier, as usual the most refined of us all, smokes his daily ration of rutabagas, spearing them on a sharp stick and turning them over a fire made of old clothes. It's a weird way to cook. I come along while he is in the midst of his smoking routine.

He says: "If you sit down, I'll slug you!"

I am surprised, and he explains: "Look there, on the ground. You see Gaston, the old farmer from Brittany. He came along just like you. He sat down, we talked about Misburg for a while, and then he stopped talking, I looked, and he was dead. It took him one second to die, no death rattle, no jerk, no nothing. Poof. Then Gaston's son comes along. The same story. He sits down, I talk to him, he dies. Then it's Father Leroy, our dear old chaplain, and the same story again. So if you don't mind, please just keep standing up."

I remain standing, thinking about these three men, all from the same region of France, who have stuck together for more than a year. They were together in prison in France, then at Compiègne, at Neuengamme, and at Misburg, and together they arrived here, at the end of the road. They died one after another only a few minutes apart, and now they're together on the other side. Probably watching us.

TYPHUS

I notice that the SS guards always stick to the roads, the main road that cuts through the camp and the one in the women's camp. I mention this to a guy who looks like he has been here for a while. He tells me there's typhus in the camp, that you get it from fleas, and that it's usually fatal. That is why there's no sign of a formal camp hierarchy.

He adds, "I'll catch it, you'll catch it, it's a matter of days. Nobody can escape it. You mustn't think about it. Thinking does no good."

The Allies had better get here fast. Otherwise, they won't find anyone left alive. So it turns out after all that these skeletal men and women didn't all die of starvation. Many of them died of typhus or some other epidemic.

A COMRADE

I'm sitting on the ground behind the huts, in a large area littered with corpses. A guy I knew at Misburg who doesn't like me shows up.

He calls out: "So there you are, you shit! I thought you dropped dead long ago!"

I reply: "No, I'm still here, as you can see. But don't worry, it won't be long!" He laughs out loud and walks away.

A RUSSIAN DIES

The women's camp is not the only place that the SS want to clear of corpses before the Allied troops arrive. There is also the men's camp. But there is no handcart. So early one morning, the guards herd us out, along with the Soviets. We move the bodies one by one, dragging them feetfirst, four inmates for each cadaver, one man for each arm and each leg. We form a long, surrealistic parade stretching from the first huts to the pit, and the parade lasts all day long. It is a pure waste of time, for completing the task would take weeks.

During one of these macabre trips, I'm tugging a right leg when a Russian, who is supposed to be pulling the left leg, falls behind. I start to shout at him. The Russian looks at me and drops dead. In an instant, like Gaston, like Father Leroy, like so many others. Now I understand why he didn't have enough strength to pull his share a minute ago. It seems there were fifteen thousand bodies still unburied when the British troops arrived. Yet we really worked hard. I can even say that I did nothing but move bodies for almost two weeks.

POW

From where I sit, I can see the SS guards outside the camp, on the other side of the fence. Some are going in and out of various buildings and loading cars. Obviously, they are about to clear out. Others, however, seem not to care about this scurrying and go on with their usual tasks. On their right arms these men are wearing white armbands, with the letters POW painted in black. I look at them with puzzlement, and then, in a flash, I understand. POW must mean "prisoner of war." These men don't feel like getting shot at. They have surrendered in advance. Our brave SS guards. They were so impressive until now.

I have wondered since whether the SS negotiated with the British command to keep us locked up in order to avoid spreading the camp diseases all over Europe, especially typhus. Everybody knows how much the British hate communicable diseases, whether it be cholera in India during the Raj or rabies today.

I now know that it is true.

THE HUNGARIANS

At about this time, I notice soldiers in yellow-brown uniforms. They replace the SS in supervising us as we drag corpses to the mass grave. They are Hungarians, doubtless troops loyal to Horthy, the Hungarian regent, who has played an ambiguous game throughout the war, both supporting and resisting Hitler. God only knows how these men got here. But they blindly obey orders.

One afternoon, after an exhausting day, a number of us are heading back down the main road toward the first set of huts. We come face-to-face with a young Hungarian who is obviously frightened by this crowd of living ghosts spilling around him on all sides. He shouts orders in his own language, but we pay no attention. Then this idiot panics and shoots at us. The two inmates ahead of me fall, one after the other. But I'm unharmed. The bullet was stopped by the second man. Then our group surges forward and the Hungarian runs away. We move slowly toward the huts, leaving the two bodies in the road. Two more.

LIBERATION

On April 15, I'm on the camp road, returning from the pit, when I hear a kind of dull roar. In the distance I see an armored vehicle with an officer on top, carrying a loudspeaker and saying I don't know what in several languages. He is a British officer. I look . . . and look again. It's hard to believe. Finally!

I sit down and hold my head in my hands. I want to cry and to laugh. I stay this way for a good while, and then I continue toward the front of the camp. The inmates I pass seem unconcerned about what is happening. For many, for most of them, it is already too late. I follow a crowd of inmates, obviously looking for food, to a warehouse, where the door has been knocked down and the contents are being looted. There's nothing here but military clothing. I find a pair of felt-lined boots that fit me. I slip them on after discarding the old pieces of ripped-up blanket I have been using as Russian footcloths as well as my disgusting shoes.

I return to the main road to see the arrival of a small column of British soldiers, rifles at the ready and an officer in the lead. They look enormously healthy and muscular by comparison with us. I remove my hat, stand to attention, and offer them my services as an interpreter. By now, I speak and understand enough German and Russian to do the job, at least for a while.

The British officer replies that, unfortunately for me, he doesn't need any help. His men are part of a fighting unit and he's going to leave soon for the front. He adds: "Besides, you won't be leaving this camp for several weeks. We need time to get organized. There's typhus here, and we don't want to be responsible for an epidemic. We have only one paramedic for sixteen men. And he has what he needs to treat wounds, but not diseases." How unprepared they are!

I don't want to stay here any longer. I plead my case, but to no avail. Finally I say, "My mother is British, her maiden name was Padwick. Before she married my father, who is a Frenchman, she lived on Carlisle Road, in East-bourne, Sussex."

This is a whopping lie: Mrs. Padwick ran a boarding-house where I spent a vacation before the war.

But it works. The officer says: "Okay, be at the camp gate this evening, and you can leave. Meanwhile, show me what there is to see here."

To see! My God!

I lead the British patrol to the edge of the pit. It isn't yet filled to the brim, far from it. But there are already thousands of bodies. The British soldiers stay there for a moment, petrified with horror, and then begin to swear. Some of them turn away to vomit.

With tears in his eyes, the officer says: "I've been fighting this war for four years, and I haven't seen anything as horrible as this. I didn't think anything like this could even exist."

As for me, I had stopped paying attention a long time ago.

SERGIO DIES

A mass of staggering inmates appears to be heading for a kind of field surrounded with barbed wire. Once there, they begin digging in the ground. Under little heaps of straw, there are potatoes. I tuck my jacket into my trousers and tighten the string that serves as my belt. I fill my jacket with potatoes, carefully buttoning it up for fear that some may fall out.

I meet Sergio on the way back to camp. I ask him for news of the others. He tells me that Ernst has died quietly and that he's lost track of Jean Gambier, who still seemed to be all right. As for Sergio himself, he's near the end, looking like a ghost. I lead him to a hut, clean out a bunk, and tuck him in under three blankets, hiding some of my potatoes under his feet. I break up some boards and build a fire outside the hut on which to cook the rest of the potatoes. I watch the fire. I watch Sergio. He smiles, wanly. I speak to him. He doesn't seem to hear. The wood has burned down to charcoal. I place my potatoes carefully on the coals. I go back into the hut. Sergio is dead.

I go out. I wonder what I'm doing still on my feet while my friends are all dying, one after the other.

Why them and not me?

LUNCH

There's a guy squatting by the fire, looking at my potatoes. He says, "You have potatoes, I have some meat, let's share." I agree. He goes off to get his meat and comes back to cook it. Suddenly I understand.

"Where did you get that meat?"

He laughs but doesn't answer.

"That has to be human flesh. I don't want any. Keep it. And I'll keep my potatoes."

He becomes furious and threatening: "You agreed to share. You can't change your mind. Even if you don't want any of my meat, you have to give me half of your potatoes."

Such is concentration camp logic. I snatch a brand out of the fire and hit him in the face with it. He runs off, screaming.

Then a woman appears, young and frail looking. She stares at my potatoes.

I ask her, in German, "Who are you?"

She replies, "A Jew."

"No, that's not what I meant. What is your nationality?"

"Austrian."

"Well, starting right now, when someone asks you, you have the right to say that you're Austrian. Please sit down and share these potatoes with me."

We leave the meat on the fire until it burns down to charcoal.

I LEAVE

Evening falls. I head for the camp gate. I catch sight of the British officer I talked to this morning and call to him. He comes to the gate, speaks to the soldiers on guard, and I walk out. Without regrets. I'm not abandoning anyone. My friends are almost all dead. I must weigh ninety or one hundred pounds, but I'm still standing. I no longer notice my repulsive filthiness or my fleas. I even have the feeling I'm quite elegant in my felt-lined boots, but I do notice that the officer keeps a fair distance between us. We go to the SS barracks, now occupied by British soldiers, in whose care the officer leaves me. He goes off, wishing me good luck.

Within myself, I feel very strong. I'm hardened, ready for anything, capable of anything. For a whole year I've worked under constant blows. I've been starved and deprived of sleep. I've been so cold I shivered from head to toe for weeks on end. I've been sick and not been treated. And I've survived.

I leave the concentration camp world believing my troubles are over. For the moment, all I can think about is eating. I am only vaguely aware that I'm going to have to unlearn everything I've learned in the camps if I am to return to civilization.

I'm not so sure that I want to.

MASS GRAVES

The pit at the end of the camp, now only half full, will be filled to the rim in the days and weeks following the camp's liberation. Other pits will be dug and filled with the skeletal bodies of wretched men and women from many countries, of many religions and nationalities. There will be no way for the British to identify them. A total of five thousand, maybe ten thousand or more, no one knows.

All across Europe, as month follows month, mothers, fathers, wives, sisters, whole families will gradually lose all hope of ever seeing their loved ones again. Then, finally, they will accept their loss. Peace be with them.

5

THE FALL

It is wise, when you are to die,
to think only of the pains and terrors
that have marked your way, of your
weariness after a long fight without other
cause than life itself, and of the need in
which you are to leave it all and rest
for a while.

THE BRITISH

The British are from the Second Army, General Dempsey commanding. They lay me on a mattress, all by myself for a change, and bring me a cup of instant tea. Marvelous British Army tea, strong and with just the right amount of milk and sugar. Put a teaspoonful in some hot water and you would think you were in England. They also give me cookies, bread, and canned food, too much canned food, unfortunately. They also bring me a big box of cigars that they found in the SS barracks, and I smoke up a storm.

They take turns sitting in my room, and we chat. In fact, I can't stop talking. I am so happy to see men who are free and healthy and to be able to speak freely. I am happy and stupid. I'm eating too much too fast, exactly like those dumb Greeks back in Misburg. But I can't help it. My hunger is too great. I can't stop eating. Once again, I have diarrhea. I go to the toilet in the hall more and more often, but it doesn't seriously bother me. This is the fourth or fifth time it has happened since I arrived in the camps, and it has always stopped by itself after a while. Otherwise, I would already be dead.

THE WAR IN THE PACIFIC

The British ask me what I will do when I go home, and I tell them that I don't want to go home, that I want to go fight the Japanese in the Pacific. They try to make me understand by gentle hints that I will first have to recover my strength, both physical and mental. Recover my strength?

I don't realize that I have become a walking skeleton and that I'm completely irrational as well. I still think I'll be back in shape in a few weeks.

In any event, I don't want to stay in Europe. If I can't fight, I'll just leave, go as far away as I can possibly go, to the end of the earth, and try to forget about my concentration camp experience among some innocent folk. I'll go to Brazil or Bali or Polynesia. In the sun, for a change. I can see myself on a beach somewhere, catching fish, collecting shells to sell to the tourists, living in a straw hut, sleeping in a hammock. I no longer need very much to live.

Just to be at peace, far from the beatings and the screaming, away from the steel-gray skies, away from uniforms and weapons, away from the piled-up corpses.

It would be wonderful.

THE F WORD

The British soldiers who were taking good care of me before they moved on constantly used a word I had never heard when spending summer holidays in Sussex with my family.

Everything was fucking: the fucking war, the fucking Germans, the fucking place, the fucking food, the fucking table, the fucking chair.

They had no fucking buddies, and I was not a fucking inmate; we were the only exceptions.

About a week later I was lying in bed when a British auxiliary girl in uniform walked in with a questionnaire of some sort to be filled out for each of us, as requested by the British authorities.

As she is leaving, I tell her how puzzled I am by an English word that I do not know: "fucking." Her face goes blank, she shrugs and walks away.

Fucking girl!

ROBBED

My British friends are gone. I'm all alone. I eat, go to the toilet, read, sleep, and wait to see what will happen next. I sleep an enormous amount. I need to catch up. At Misburg, what with all the alerts and the actual bombing raids, I must have averaged five hours a night.

One day the door opens. A concentration camp inmate enters. He's tall and strong. He inspects the room and then snatches one of my blankets and starts piling everything the British left me on top of it. All the canned the food, the newspapers. He even takes my felt-lined boots. He works calmly, methodically before my eyes. I don't open my mouth. I let him get on with it. I don't even look at him. I no longer have the strength to fight him.

He ties a knot in the full blanket, slings it over his shoulder, and leaves, still cool and collected. There's nothing left for me to do but go back to sleep.

DELOUSED

The days pass. I can't stay alone in this room indefinitely. I have nothing to eat, and I need medicine to stop the diarrhea. I go out, hugging the walls for support. Someone notices me, and I'm taken to a big delousing center. They take off all my clothes and burn them. They wash me from head to toe and spray me with DDT. I find myself clean again, deloused, and lying on a pallet on the floor in a large room with other inmates in the same decrepit state as I'm in. We are still eating British army rations, mostly canned food. I grow weaker from day to day. It's getting hard simply to drag myself to the bucket. Food passes straight through my digestive system.

MAY 8

I'm dozing on my pallet when a terrible racket awakens me. All the guns in the area are firing at the same time. My first thought is that the war has started again, but I see the British going about their business as if nothing were happening. I stick an arm out from under my blanket and catch a passing British soldier by the leg of his pants. I ask him why all the noise. He bursts out laughing. It's a great day! VE day! The end of the war in Europe.

I sob under the covers for some time. I think of my brother, of all those who failed to make it to this day, of my comrades, my "brothers in misery," as Vladimir called them. I envy them in a way. For them, the struggle is ended. I don't have much strength left or much willpower. I can't even raise my blankets any longer by flexing my legs, nor turn on my side. I wonder whether perhaps I'm going to join the others very soon.

THE POLISH WOMEN

The British are getting organized. After a few days, they carry me to a big barrack, into a room with iron bedsteads and mattresses, blankets and night tables. They put me in a corner near an open window, along with another inmate whose foot sticks out from under his bedding. I talk to him, but he doesn't answer. He doesn't seem to hear. At this point, a group of Polish women inmates appears, handing out vitamins. They are in robust health, so they must certainly have been part of the concentration camp ruling class. They seem confident, and they chatter like magpies.

I ask them for some extra vitamins, which they refuse to give me, and I insult them profusely in their own language. They answer me in the same spirit, slam the door, and lock it behind them. I'm alone again with the dying man. I have food and drink on my night table, but I don't want it. I decide to try to calm my agitated intestines by fasting for a few days. I have no idea what else I could do.

THE GLASSES

Several days go by like this. I sleep a lot. I neither eat nor drink. I wait. The silent guy has died. It has been some time since the foot sticking out from his covers stopped moving, and his flesh has gone gray, though the smell isn't very strong yet. No one has come into the room. The Polish women may have thrown the key away. From time to time, someone tries the door but gives up. I wait.

At a certain point, I make a desperate effort to sit up, holding onto the head of the bed for leverage. Then I see my reflection in a windowpane. I can scarcely recognize myself, so drastically have I changed. My skin has contracted into my eye-sockets, creating some sort of spectacles around my eyes. I've seen this a number of times before, on Sergio, for example, and it's a certain omen. It means I'm finished. At most I have a few days left. Now I know what I'm waiting for. I am waiting for death, and I have accepted death for some time now. I let my body slump back to a lying position. I am calm, perfectly calm. No more struggle, no more fighting against this stubborn diarrhea. I will soon be rid of this worn-out rag of a body.

I wait this way for hours. I have no fear. Time seems to drag on. I'm bored. Finally, night falls. I'm in the dark and I fall asleep. I wake up the next morning in full daylight. I wiggle my fingers, open and close my eyes. I'm still alive. I start waiting once again, but nothing happens. My heart beats, I breathe, my stomach rumbles. I have the feeling that my death scene is taking too long, and I don't understand why. In the case of my friends, things always went much faster. But after all, there's nothing I can do about it. The day passes interminably. Night comes, and I fall asleep again. I don't care whether I die in my sleep. I'd like to get this over with as soon as possible. On the table next to my bed lies a card the British authorities gave me, with my name and nationality:

DISPLACED PERSON INDEX CARD
G 01708058

At least my family will be notified, even if my body stays in Germany.

WALTER

I wake up again at first light. I am in despair. If I can't go on living and I can't die, what can I do? I start waiting again. And then a key turns in the lock. A German enters, wearing the uniform of the army medical service, carrying a bucket of milk and a dipper. He's a POW who has been let out in order to care for the concentration camp survivors. He walks up to the quiet guy's bed and immediately turns away. He sits on the bed next to mine, near the window, and notices all the food on my night table.

"So, you're not eating?"

"No, I'm not hungry. I have diarrhea. Leave me alone."

"No, I won't leave you alone. If you don't eat, you'll die."

"I don't care."

"Dying now would be too stupid. The war's over."

"I don't give a damn."

"You're an asshole, a real asshole. You don't realize how lucky we are, you and me, to be alive today, after a war that's killed such an enormous number of people on all sides."

"I'm fed up! I've had this diarrhea for a month. I'm at the end of my rope. Let me die in peace. Please go away."

"No! I won't let you die stupidly. I'm going to look after you."

Walter holds up my head and spoon-feeds me milk for quite a while. I let him do what he wants. I don't give a damn. Then he leaves with his bucket and dipper, telling me he'll be back. A couple of hours later he does come back and carries me easily in his arms to another room, where there are three other concentration camp inmates. They must be in reasonably good shape, since they get up from time to time. One of them is an Austrian, a professional soccer player. Walter tells the other patients to look after me and to call him if things go wrong.

I am no longer alone now. I am no longer abandoned.

THE SWISS DOCTOR

A little fellow in a dark suit shows up in the room and starts to examine me in earnest. He takes my pulse, listens to my heartbeat, my breathing. It's been a month since the British forces liberated Bergen-Belsen, and he is the first doctor I've seen, a Swiss. I give him a big speech about Switzerland's humanitarian role in wartime, about neutrality, about Swiss orderliness, Swiss cleanliness, Swiss sobriety. I'm on a real high. He gives me medicine to take regularly. Over my head, hanging from the window knob, he sets up a large bottle of plasma for a transfusion. I learn later that the plasma comes from Australia, and I will be able to say with a certain amount of pride that I have Australian blood in my veins. The doctor takes a big gold watch from his vest pocket and carefully times the drip mechanism. Then he leaves.

I watch distractedly as the drops fall from the bottle, one after the other. After a while, I start fiddling with the valve. I speed up, then slow down the flow. I close it off or open it up all the way. So finally, when my dear doctor returns, there's nothing left in the bottle. He is appalled and starts to bawl me out, going so far as to say, "You know this could have killed you."

"So what?"

He leaves, shaking his head. But he will be back to see me, always very serious, always very conscientious. He may never know it, but, along with Walter, he gave me the courage to come out of my hole and continue to struggle, the courage to want to go on living on this earth.

THE GERMAN DOCTOR

Some time after that, a German doctor in uniform shows up. He is a POW, like Walter, and, like Walter, he has been released from camp by the British, who apparently do not have enough doctors of their own. He examines me and questions me, but his uniform brings back terrible memories, which was not the case with Walter because of his extreme kindness.

I tell him, "You're not the one to ask questions around here. I am."

I speak with such vehemence that he stands to attention.

"I have chronic diarrhea," I say, "caused by the return to a rich diet, mostly canned goods. What medicines do you have?"

He names a certain medicine. And I ask, "What is the normal dose?"

"Two a day, one in the morning, one at night."

"Fine. We'll try the normal dose for three days. If that doesn't work, we'll double the dose, up to four pills a day. And if that doesn't work, we'll go to eight a day, then sixteen. Then, if that doesn't work, we'll stop and try another medicine."

He looks at me in disbelief and then, like a good German, follows my orders. We go through this routine with several German medicines with no significant result, but also without doing any great damage to my system. The diarrhea continues.

THE SOVIET MARSHALS

A British soldier gave me an old magazine featuring page after page of color pictures of Soviet marshals: Zhukov, Konev, Malinovsky, Rokosovsky, as well as several other magnificent warriors in full-dress uniform with banks of medals on their chests. Three Soviet inmates show up in our room, and I give them the magazine. They tell me that they are organizing themselves for their forthcoming return home and that these portraits will decorate the walls of the place they use as an office.

Through them, I learn that the British military authorities have decreed that German farmers must provide food to all passing foreigners. Hundreds of thousands of what are called "displaced persons" are now returning home on foot, by stages, without waiting for the authorities to arrange to repatriate them. They are only the healthy ones, skilled workers and ex-POWs. My Soviet friends take advantage of the British order to get provisions from the neighboring farms. They offer me a chicken and some eggs, which I have no way of cooking, so I refuse them.

Much later, it was said that all the returning Soviets were executed on arrival or sent to Siberia. Yet some of them had displayed true heroism, especially the partisans, who carried out effective military actions behind the German lines. But in the Red Army any officer, noncom, or soldier who was taken prisoner by the enemy was regarded as a deserter and treated as such. And then, Stalin did not want his socialist paradise to be contaminated by people who had seen other ways of life. He was not interested in their courage, loyalty, or even heroism.

THE LIAISON OFFICER

Walter comes to tell me that there is a French officer in the hallway who is checking the identity of his fellow countrymen in order to send them home. It is the end of May, and I have not yet been in touch with my family. For some time now I have realized it will take me months to recover physically and that there is nowhere I can possibly go except to my parents' home. I ask Walter to tell the officer to see me.

Henri François-Poncet appears in the room. I recognize him right away, but he doesn't recognize me. I remind him of a party I attended at his parents' house in the Champs de Mars section of Paris, before the war, when his father André was the French ambassador to Berlin. We chat for a while. He is returning to Paris in a few days and promises to telephone my family right away. My dreams of tropical beaches fade away.

THE FRENCH RED CROSS

The French Red Cross had formed intensive-care teams of doctors and paramedics with trucks full of medicine and predigested food. Just what we needed. The Red Cross official in charge of the missing persons department called up a British general in Brussels around April 20 and offered to put these teams at the general's disposal. He was told that the British army had no use for them. So the trained technicians who made up those teams spent the spring of 1945 playing volleyball at Arcachon, on the Atlantic coast near Bordeaux, while concentration camp inmates who were still alive when the camps were liberated died day after day, week after week. Thousands and thousands of them.

MY MOTHER

A week later, my mother arrives. I don't know how she did it, but she has somehow managed to come all the way here. She is wearing the uniform she wore as a volunteer nurse in a surgical unit during World War I. She gives me a sad little smile and takes me in her arms. I don't realize what kind of an impression I must be making on her, skeletal and overexcited as I am. I also have a high fever. And the British authorities don't want to let me leave, still out of fear that I might start an epidemic. My mother has to fill out endless forms and sign a formal discharge before they finally give in. She will nurse me for months and bring me back to life, only to die herself at age fifty-three, a delayed victim of the pain and hardship of the war.

CELLE

Walter and another man place me on a stretcher and go down the stairs singing, my mother bringing up the rear. Walter, who has nursed the wounded for five years of war and is now caring for us, is joyful, carefree, delighted to be alive. I shake his hand with great emotion before my stretcher is loaded into an ambulance to go to the airstrip at Celle, a small airport between Hamburg and Hanover.

I'm unloaded onto the tarmac beside an old Junker 52. It's a three-engine German plane made of corrugated iron, with huge red crosses painted on its sides. Beside me, on his own two legs, is another former inmate from Misburg, Bob the electrician, whom I detest. There is a lot of ill will between us. He claims that he was turned in to the Gestapo by a friend of mine in the Resistance who, he says, broke down under Nazi torture, a charge I refuse to believe.

Bob has a certain amount of technical skill, so the camp boss put him in charge of the lighting, as well as the electrified fences, at Misburg. He also used electrodes to rig up a water-heating system to supply baths for the concentration camp hierarchy. He has had typhus and an abscess. He is pale and haggard, with popping eyes and an enormous scar on his neck and jaw.

He says to my mother, "Ah, Madame Renouard, Jean-Pierre is my best friend."

Upon which I say, "Don't pay attention, Mother. He's completely delirious."

My mother is confused but says nothing.

The British have pinned a card to my blanket. It says:

FIELD MEDICAL CARD
Bergen-Belsen Concentration Camp
Diagnosis: Starvation

They might have added: "Followed by overeating."

THE EIFFEL TOWER

The plucky little Junker isn't soundproof. Its three engines make a lot of noise, it vibrates, it pitches and tosses. Lying on my stretcher, I watch the landscape rushing by outside the plane. We're not flying very high. I can see France, its fields, its villages, its church steeples, the France I came so close to never seeing again. I think of what my surroundings have been for the past year: the barracks, the camp squares, the electrified barbed-wire fences, the watchtowers. I think of Germany under the bombing, its harshness, its discipline, its inhumanity, the Nazi Germany from which I am flying away. We approach the great Parisian metropolis and I see the Eiffel Tower in the distance. I finally accept the obvious fact that the Nazi's concentration camp universe has ceased to exist, that it lives on only in our bruised bodies and in our deranged minds.

Those of us who are returning will try, the best we can, to recover. We are going to have to live. We are going to have to try to forget and forgive. I don't know whether we will be able to do it.

The Junker lands, and they remove my stretcher. My father is on the landing strip. He is wearing a black armband in memory of my brother. His ravaged face reflects infinite sadness. He kisses my mother, and together they look at their only remaining son, at this feverish body, this lunatic face smiling at them.

Thank you, Adolf.

6

AFTERMATH

November 1945. After seven months of illness, typhoid fever, phlebitis, pleurisy, pulmonary embolism, I begin to walk again. At the beginning, someone had to move my feet for me, one after the other, but now I can manage it on my own. I decide to go out. I take a bath, I shave. I find just about everything I need in the cupboards among my father's and my cousin's clothes. I put on a clean shirt, a tie, a jacket. I look at myself in the mirror. My hair, though still dull looking, has grown and now almost completely hides the nape-to-forehead shaved skull that was the standard haircut in the concentration camp.

I take a taxi and go the Champs Elysées, the great avenue of downtown Paris. I start walking slowly. For the first time in two years, I walk a distance of more than a hundred yards without a guard pointing his rifle at my back. I turn around instinctively to make sure. I sit down at a sidewalk cafe and watch people pass by: soldiers, boys and girls, older people. They talk among themselves. They laugh. They look happy. I feel that I'm different from them, a complete stranger. I still belong to the concentration camp world.

I think of my brother and of all the friends who never made it back. Sergio, Ernst, Gilbert, Etoc, and the others.

I should be with them. Here I am, lost and lonely. I could talk about it only with those who shared that terrible year at Neuengamme, at Misburg, and at Belsen. A few are still alive: Jean Gambier, Bernard Morey, Jean Mattéoli. But they are scattered, taking up the interrupted threads of their lives. Except for them, no one can understand.

THE HOTEL SUISSE

December 1945. I am in a rest center for returning concentration camp inmates, prisoners of war, and Nazi victims. It is the Hotel Suisse at Chamonix, a French ski resort in the Alps. I join a group that always eats at the same table, each at his own place.

Because there are no ashtrays, I get into the habit of leaning back in my chair and crushing my butts on the wall, then dropping them on the floor. I am very surprised, when I go to check out, that the proprietor scolds me for my behavior and asks to be reimbursed for the damage to her wall. I pay up.

And she says: "You know, sir, you don't just put out cigarettes on a wall."

I reply: "I'm sorry. I didn't realize I was doing it."

To which she responds with a pitying look: "I can well believe that!"

THE SUBWAY

February 1946. I get around Paris on the Métro, the city's old subway system. But travelling in the Métro produces a kind of throbbing in my head. The subway cars all look alike, the stations look alike, the sounds are always the same, when the train is running, when it stops, when it starts up again. In the end, I am lost. I can't recall where I was going, what day it is, whether it's morning or afternoon. I have to get out to the street level, sit on a bench, and wait for my head to clear. It seems this is what is called amnesia. I don't know whether it is due to the nervous shock of repeated bombings or the starvation in the camps. I decide not to mention it to anyone and to write everything down in a notebook.

GERMAN ORDERLINESS

One day, I go to a designated police station in Paris and file a formal complaint against the SS organization for taking my personal belongings when I arrived in Neuengamme. Several months later, I receive an equally formal reply: "We have recovered a number of personal objects belonging to you." I ask that they be sent on, and one day I receive a small rectangular package containing my watch, its face dark with dust and the leather strap shrivelled up with age, the cross I received at baptism and its gold chain, and the silver fountain pen I was given for my first Communion. I go to a watchmaker, but he says my watch cannot be repaired. I throw it away. The cross and chain will be stolen from me later, in a burglary. I still have the pen, an old-fashioned model that has to be filled with an eyedropper. A gift from my godmother.

THE FROZEN PIPES

It is winter 1947. As I was last winter, I'm always too hot. I walk frequently in the woods around Paris wearing nothing but a shirt, no sweater, no coat. I don't mind the rain or the snow. In the big run-down house where I live with my father, it's the same thing. I keep my own room and bathroom ice-cold, with the radiators turned off and the windows wide open. I wash in cold water. I am perfectly happy, perfectly comfortable until the day when water no longer flows from the faucet. I go to my father's overheated bathroom and turn on the tap. Water flows. My father then returns the visit, wrapping up warmly before he enters my bathroom. He looks around, tries the faucet, and finally says, "Your pipes are frozen, son. If you want to wash, you're going to have to close the window and turn on the radiator."

Then, noticing my glum face, he adds, "At least for a few days."

THE TRAIN

I am going to Sweden by train through Germany. The glass and iron roofs of railway stations in big German cities that were destroyed in the Allied bombing raids have not yet been replaced. The huge metal columns, now supporting nothing at all, look like lopped-off palm trees planted at regular intervals along the platforms. When my international train stops in a German station, blinds are drawn down over the dining-car windows so that the foreign travellers comfortably eating their big meals cannot be seen by the Germans, who still have precious little to eat. When a porter forgets to draw the blinds, the Germans throw stones at the windows.

The train is moving now, and I come back from the dining car. While I was away eating, a German has sat in my reserved seat. I smoke a cigarette in the corridor and then I enter the compartment. I say to the interloper what the camp bosses used to say when they wanted me to move, something like, "Haul your ass, man." He rises as if someone has struck him and leaves. One thing is sure: I will have to make as little use as possible of the German I picked up in the concentration camp.

KATYN

In Stockholm, I meet a Swedish diplomat who closely followed the recent war and knows a great deal about it. He reminds me that some five thousand Polish officers were massacred at Katyn in 1941.

"Did you know," he asks me, "that over the mass grave where those poor fellows were buried, trees were planted that had to be uprooted to get to the bodies?

"In the region there are many other older trees, all about the same age planted in clumps of several hundred. It is likely that they mark other mass graves that will probably never be opened and that contain the bodies of God only knows whom.

"Using all the resources of their huge propaganda machine, the Soviets have disclaimed responsibility for Katyn and placed the blame for the massacre on Hitler's special troops. But the technique of the executions was typically Soviet. The victims' hands were tied behind their backs and they were killed with a single shot in the back of the neck. This is typical of the NKVD, who apparently own the land. There is no doubt who the real killers were."

THE PICNIC

1948. I have met Monique, a pure and beautiful girl, just out of a Catholic school. We are deeply in love. Every day, she sees the lingering marks the camps have left on me: my insensitivity to cold, the way I literally gobble up my food, finishing even the tiniest crumb of bread. Also, and most horrifying, she learns of my sudden roaring fits of anger, which don't last long but are terrible. She's frightened and appalled.

We are making sandwiches for a picnic with friends when I cut my finger deeply. I burst out laughing as I watch the blood pour out on the tiled kitchen floor, and I stroll over to the sink, where I let the blood drip away as I go on talking to Monique. After a few minutes I shake my finger, run a little water to remove the coagulated blood, and rinse out the sink. I bind my finger in my handkerchief. Monique suggests disinfecting the wound and making a real dressing. She speaks sweetly and seriously, but something suddenly clicks in my head and I start screaming at the top of my voice in German, involuntarily imitating Hermann and the other camp bosses. Monique runs off, and the picnic never takes place.

Later I beg her pardon, I see her again. She becomes my wife against the wishes of her family, who are afraid of me and who doubt that I can make her happy. It will take a very long time for Hermann, Winter, and the rest of them to disappear from my life. My children will get to know them as wicked spirits who took possession of their daddy at the most unexpected moments, who screamed in an unknown language and filled them with fear.

MEETING IN BORDEAUX

1952. With an American colleague, I am making a business trip in southwest France. We stop in Bordeaux, where the regional director of our company takes us to lunch at a restaurant on the Cours de l'Intendance, one of the main streets of town. It is the very street where during the war there was a big German-language bookstore. I used to watch young submarine officers in uniform, wearing their dress daggers on their belts, go in and buy reading matter before diving back into the Atlantic.

We talk business, but I feel ill at ease. I don't know why. Then, at a certain point, I turn to our waiter and ask for mineral water. It's Bob the electrician. His eyes are less weary looking, but he still has the jagged scar on his cheek and neck. I turn away, and he goes on serving lunch in the normal way. Once I'm outside, I heave a sigh of relief. The others haven't noticed anything, and I don't say a word.

PETER O'NEILL

1955. I am in Saigon, playing golf with an American about my age. We then retire to the club bar and chat over our iced drinks; it's very hot. Peter is a tall, amiable fellow. He tells me he fought in Europe as a tail gunner in a bomber. I mention Misburg and describe the bombing raids on the refinery.

He laughs and says: "I bombed Misburg on November 26. I didn't know you were down there, or I promise I would have dropped my bombs somewhere else."

Later, we play another round of golf.

No hard feelings.

THE RUSSIAN NIGHTCLUB

A couple I know from San Francisco is in Paris. They are rich Americans who have taken a suite in one of the best hotels. She is Austrian born, a brunette with blue eyes, lovely. She lost her whole family in the gas chambers and has never gone back to Vienna. The three of us dine together several evenings in a row at very good restaurants and drink a lot. Tonight we are at a Russian nightclub. The show starts with Russian folk songs, songs I've heard a hundred times. Songs that recall the camps and move me deeply. We talk about the war, the concentration camps, and unwittingly I say to the woman: "My dear, if I had been a young German instead of a young Frenchman, I would have fought in the war, and I don't like to think of the kind of orders I might have been asked to carry out."

She looks at me and begins to cry: "How can you say that after all you went through?"

I couldn't explain. She would never understand. I left with a heavy heart, and I never saw those friends again.

THE RANCH

I am in Texas, not far from Fort Worth. I lean on a rail fence and watch the cowboys driving cattle from one pen to another with a lot of whistling and shouting. The scene reminds me of the concentration camp inmates in barrack II rushing outside, propelled by blows and curses from Hermann and Mishka. The sound of their wooden soles clopping on the cement as they flee to the door, backs bent, then the scrum at the door itself. I feel as though I were still there.

Yet all that was very long ago, very far away. I make an effort to think of something else.

THE DRIVER

1975–1980. I work a lot with Germans, and I often go to Frankfurt and Düsseldorf. I also go to Hamburg. Everyone is nice, the secretaries bring me coffee all day long, and the executives take me to lunch at the best restaurants. Everyone speaks English. In the limousine on the way to the airport, I ask the driver for a map of the city and its suburbs. He fishes a map out of the glove compartment. I see that Neuengamme is not far away. I do not, however, ask to be taken there, although I have time to spare.

THE SOVIET PARTISANS' SONG

> From the mountains and the plains,
> The cities and the farms,
> When the great Lenin called,
> The partisans rose up.

1977. Several executives and I travel regularly to Moscow to negotiate the purchase of raw materials from the Soviets. Today we are in a sports club just below the Kremlin walls. We emerge from the sauna, naked under our big Turkish towels. We chat over beers, which, because we are so dehydrated, go straight to our heads. One of our Soviet friends, Lev, was in the second tank of Marshal Zhukov's army to enter Berlin in 1945. He tells everyone who cares to listen that he, personally, liberated me.

"No, Lev," I protest, "you never got past Berlin. It was the British army who liberated me."

"No," Lev insists. "I tell you it was me, it was the Red Army which defeated the Nazis from Stalingrad to Berlin. If it weren't for the Red Army, you'd still be in your camp."

Thus begins a drunken conversation that ends only when we break into song together, Lev in Russian, I in French. We sing the song of the partisans and exchange fraternal kisses on the cheek. Ever since, Lev has continued to claim that it was he who liberated me. Dear old Lev.

SÃO PAOLO

It is 1979. At the baggage claim in the São Paolo airport, the one in the middle of town that serves Brazil's internal lines, I'm waiting for my suitcase. A tall man, very erect, with close-cropped hair, is waiting beside me. His icy blue eyes remind me of something. But what?

He has the eyes of an SS man, completely devoid of human feeling. He also has the look and behavior of the SS, and his clothes indicate that he lives here in Brazil. He retrieves his bag and leaves. I will never know who he is or what he may have done during the war.

In any case, there are a lot of Nazis in South America. One of my friends from Argentina once told me that after the war, five German submarines were found abandoned on a beach in the south of the country. There was no one on board, no luggage, just dirty plates and refuse.

A large number of SS officers and camp guards scattered before the liberation. It took years of searching to find a few of the most notorious, and they were judged only twenty or thirty, even forty years after the events.

Those who were captured at the liberation were dealt with the best the Allies could manage, for most of the witnesses of their crimes had joined the victims on the piles of corpses in the camps or had gone home as human wrecks. The little guys, those who were simply cogs in the concentration camp system, got off free.

The Allies showed even fewer scruples when they killed tens of thousands of civilians in bombing raids on German cities, Berlin, Dresden, Hanover, Hamburg, and other cities that emerged from the war as yards-deep piles of rubble.

THE GAS STATION

I return home late one night and stop at one of the few gas stations that are still open. I get out of the car as the attendant is replacing the cap on the gas tank. I notice that he is a Cambodian. I once lived in his country for a few years, so I address a few words to him in his own language. He is a refugee who survived the slaughter carried out by Pol Pot and the Khmer Rouge. I can see the traces of horror and terror in his eyes, in his face. Like me, he's an ex–concentration camp inmate, but younger, more recent.

We speak about Cambodia as it was before the war, of its beauty and its peace, of the strong and happy Khmer and of the murderous folly that has decimated them. He weeps. I take his hands in mine and weep with him, the two of us alone in the suburban night, united like brothers.

It does him good. He gets control of himself. I give him a big tip and get back on the road.

Will all this never end?

THE CREMATORIUM

The Neuengamme crematorium was used frequently. It emitted thick black smoke, even denser than the smoke from the burning Misburg gas tanks.

It is the morning of April 15, 1985, forty years to the day from when the British liberated Bergen-Belsen. I am crossing the Seine on the Puteaux Bridge, heading for La Défense, the modern new "office city" to the west of Paris. Near the bridge is a hospital complex, and from the hospital chimney pours black smoke, just like that at Neuengamme. And no one notices.

None of these men on the way to their offices, already thinking of their business or listening to their car radios or cassettes, none of these men sees anything but thick, black smoke, and it revives in them no memories.

THE PILGRIMAGE

Today there is a large parking lot in front of Bergen-Belsen and a wall along which you walk to get to the site of the camp. Every trace of the camp itself has disappeared. What remains is a vast clearing with birch trees and heather, surrounded by the deep and soundless forest. Not a single bird lives here. Along the twisting main road of what was once the camp, there is one mass grave after another, each topped by a mound of earth about three feet high and marked with a gravestone inscribed with the approximate number of bodies, two thousand, three thousand, five thousand, and so on. As you walk along this path, a growing anguish stifles you. No one can get all the way to the monument at the end of the road without being overcome by sobs. Yet all is calm, all is serene. But the earth has been forever impregnated by the misery, by the suffering, by the agony of so many.

This land is cursed, like Auschwitz, like Treblinka and the other extermination camps. This land can never again be anything but a place of pilgrimage for those who cannot forget.

THE RESTAURANT

My wife and I are invited by a German couple to dine with them in one of the most expensive restaurants of the capital. He is a businessman my age, the owner of a large chemical company that he created after the war. He is hugely rich. When I suggest that he might wish to see our Impressionist paintings at the Musée d'Orsay, he answers, "I am only interested in paintings that I can buy, and those you speak of are not for sale."

All day long he drinks the best champagne, as he has for a long time, so that now his hands shake constantly.

He does not know that I have spent time in the camps, and I have no intention of telling him, just as I do not ask him what he did during the war. We have a good business relationship, that's all.

Once he looked at me and raised his glass: "Dear Monsieur Renouard, let's drink to our generation of men who built Europe on the ruins of the war."

We clink glasses and I drink with him, as I should, but a bit pensively nevertheless, thinking that he was a German, I was a Frenchman, and now we are Europeans. For better or worse, through thick and thin. *Durch dick und dünn.*

EPILOGUE

I have never understood why I was privileged to come out alive from the Nazi death camps, then to recover, get married, father children, work successfully, and go on and on until today.

Of course I had guts. I was determined and resilient, but no more so than many who did not make it. Also, I was lucky. "You have the luck you deserve," Colonel Groussard told me once, and he meant it. He was the head of French military intelligence.

I was young, adventurous, unattached. I was prepared to die. It was so common, if only in the guns pointed at us. When things were really bad, it would have been a relief to join my ancestors, my brother, and so many of my friends in another world.

There should have been purpose. I don't believe that someone upstairs was spinning a wheel and that my number came out. What the purpose was, I still don't know. It may be that the yogis have the answer to this one. They would say with a smile that I had agreed beforehand to cleanse myself in one go of all the bad karma accumulated over many lifetimes. They would say that once I was a Japanese warrior, a Samurai who lived by the sword, later a Mayan priest in the Yucatán who sacrificed one victim after another to comfort the bleeding evening sun god. They would say that this time I was to learn the lessons of misery, suffering, despair, forgiveness. This I have done so that I could be free.

Now there is this book, which is for the young ones, particularly my children, Ophélie, Philippe, and Sophie, and their children and grandchildren. I hope that it may help them understand the folly of war and the greatness of man when day after day he has to go beyond his own limits or die.

The horror was in many lands: in Nazi Germany, in Stalin's Siberia, in Japanese camps. It is with us now, on a smaller scale, but one day it will end when man will have changed for the better.